Microwave
Cuisine

A BAY BOOKS PUBLICATION
An imprint of HarperCollinsPublishers

First published in Australia in 1988 by Bay Books
This edition published in 1992

Bay Books, of
CollinsAngus&Robertson Publishers Pty Limited
A division of HarperCollinsPublishers (Australia) Pty Limited
25 Ryde Road, Pymble NSW 2073, Australia

HarperCollinsPublishers (New Zealand) Limited
31 View Road, Glenfield, Auckland 10, New Zealand

HarperCollinsPublishers Limited
77– 85 Fulham Palace Road, London W6 8JB, United Kingdom

Copyright © Joan McDermott

National Library of Australia
Card Number and ISBN 1 86378 065 3

Photography: Lennard Osbeck
Food styling: Christa Osbeck
Designed by Ivy Hansen
Typeset by Savage Type Pty Ltd, Brisbane
Printed in Australia by Griffin Press, Adelaide

5 4 3 2
95 94 93 92

Microwave Cuisine

For Microwave and
Microwave Convection Ovens

Joan McDermott

BayBooks
An imprint of HarperCollins*Publishers*

CONTENTS

INTRODUCTION

This book has been designed to provide the kind of practical information that usually takes years of experience to accumulate. It covers both the do's and don'ts of microwave and microwave/convection cooking, together with recipes for both types of ovens.

All the microwave recipes in this book have been tested in ovens with a 650 watt output. Wattage on domestic microwave ovens varies between 500 and 750 watts, so it may be necessary to vary the cooking times slightly depending on the wattage of your oven.

Refer to your manufacturer's manual to determine the wattage of your oven. If you have a 500 watt oven it is best to cook for the times specified. Then, if necessary, add approximately 10% of the cooking time again. 700/750 watt ovens may need reduced times.

Combination and convection recipes have been tested in the Panasonic Dimension 4 (9807), Sharp Exceller (R 8560) and Sanyo 5710 ovens. These are all cyclic combination ovens. As a guideline, owners of Toshiba combination ovens should use the timings provided for Sharp. Westinghouse combination owners should follow Panasonic timings.

HOW MICROWAVE OVENS WORK

Microwaves are non-ionising electro-magnetic waves within a particular frequency band, similar to radio waves. They are produced by a magnetron usually concealed in the roof of the oven and enter the oven through a guide channel.

Microwaves bounce off the metal walls of the oven cavity until they are absorbed by the moisture molecules in food. They enter food from the outside, causing friction between the moisture molecules which in turn produces heat. They then cook by conduction from the outside to the centre.

Microwaves transmit through glass, china, plastic and paper. They are reflected off any metal surface so the inside cavity of the oven is always metal. Some ovens have a stainless steel finish, others are finished with a white epoxy. Every microwave manufacturer has to adhere to stringent safety standards set at an international level. All microwave ovens have a metal screen in the door and safety locking devices designed to prevent microwave leakage.

As you would change the temperature on a conventional oven, you can change the power setting on a microwave oven. Some ovens have more power settings than others. These levels can include defrost, low, medium-low, medium, medium-high and high.

Each power level represents the percentage of time microwave energy is present in the oven. If the microwave oven is operating on a high power setting, this is usually referred to as 100% of microwave power being present in the oven. If it is operating on a medium power level, the bursts of microwave energy would be the same but there

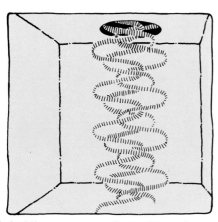

1. Microwaves are directed into the oven cavity by the wave guide.

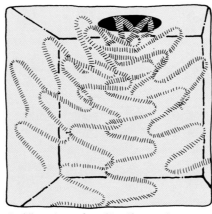

2. The stirrer fan distributes the waves. Some models also have a turntable to rotate food.

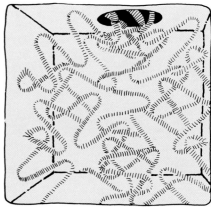

3. Microwaves are randomly deflected off metal oven walls. This promotes even cooking.

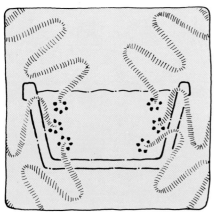

4. The waves penetrate the food to a depth of about 2 cm.

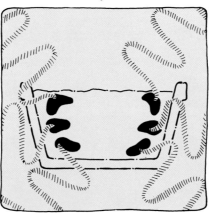

5. They produce friction which creates heat which cooks the food.

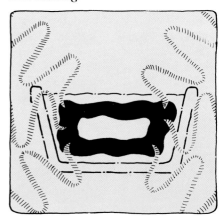

6. Heat spreads to the centre by conduction. Stir or turn food for even cooking.

would be breaks between the bursts, so microwave energy would be present only 50% of the time. Therefore the power level is called 50%. The longer the break between bursts of microwave energy, the lower the power level.

Different manufacturers call their microwave power levels by different names. If a microwave recipe refers to medium power, it may not necessarily mean medium on your oven. Therefore it is necessary to know the percentage of microwave power represented by each of your power settings.

In this book, each recipe includes the name of the power setting followed by the percentage of power this name most commonly represents; for example high (100%) or medium (50%). If in doubt, it's always best to cook by percentage.

Refer to your manufacturer's manual or our chart to learn the percentages of power for your microwave oven. Once you know them you will be able to use any cookbook accurately.

As new microwave oven models come on the market, you may need to experiment and adjust the timings given in this book. Always undercook, test, and if necessary, cook a few seconds more.

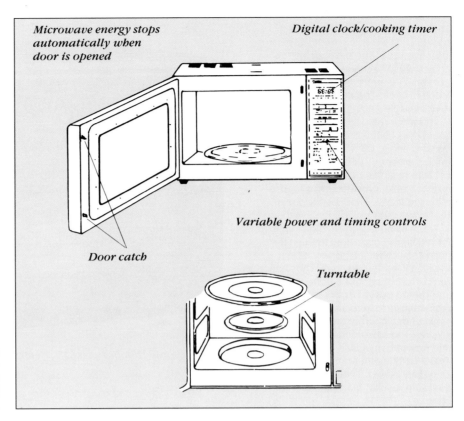

Microwave energy stops automatically when door is opened

Digital clock/cooking timer

Variable power and timing controls

Door catch

Turntable

POWER % CHART

POWER %	PANASONIC	SANYO	SHARP	PHILIPS	TOSHIBA	WESTINGHOUSE
100%	High	100%	High	Full cook high	High 9	High
90%	Medium-high	90%				Medium-high
80%		80%			8	
70%	Medium	70%	Medium-high	Medium-high Roast	Medium-high 7	Medium
60%		60%			6	
50%	Medium-low	50%	Medium	Simmer stew Medium	Medium 5	Medium-low
40%		40%			4	
35% 30%	Defrost Low	30%	Medium-low Defrost	Medium-low Defrost	Medium-low 3	Defrost Low
20%		20%			2	
10%	Warm	10%	Low		1	Warm
0%	Stand	0%				Stand

MICROWAVE/CONVECTION OVENS

The microwave/convection or combination oven is a dream come true. No longer does the devoted microwave cook have to sacrifice quality for convenience or have a limited choice of foods to cook. The best of both worlds is now available.

When operated as a normal microwave oven, the principles of microwave cooking apply. Do not use plates with a gold or silver rim, or deep metal containers as they will cause arcing. Foil is acceptable, provided more food is exposed than foil and the foil doesn't touch any metal components in the oven.

When using the convection cycle, fan-forced heat is circulated through the oven in much the same way as in a traditional fan-forced oven. Conventional recipes can be cooked using this cycle. Fan-forced ovens usually cook slightly more quickly than radiant ovens, so you may need to shorten the cooking times slightly. The convection element in a microwave/convection oven is less than 1600 watts, compared to 2400 watts in an ordinary oven. This means it produces the same results, but is cheaper to operate.

Microwave/convection ovens usually fall into two categories.

The Panasonic Dimension 4 (9807) oven

A selection of combination oven dishes

Dual or simultaneous ovens use both microwave energy and convection heat circulated by hot air blown over an element. For safety reasons, these ovens usually use only 600 watts output on the microwave cycle. The temperature range is between 130°C and 250°C and the user can sometimes select how much microwave power and how much convectional heat to use.

Cyclic ovens use microwave energy and convection heat alternately rather than simultaneously. The oven switches from one mode to the other throughout the cooking process. The operation of this cycle differs with each manufacturer. Most of these ovens operate by using pre-programmed combinations of microwave and convectional heat. Some ovens offer more than one combination setting designed for use with different food types. Some also have the flexibility of being able to alter the convection temperature required.

The majority of microwave/convection ovens currently on the market are cyclic ovens, which is why we have chosen to test our recipes in a cyclic oven.

Sources of heat can also differ. They fall into three categories which are combined with microwave power:

☐ Fan-forced conventional heat which is air forced over an element by using a fan.

☐ Double flat bed elements, one situated on the roof of the oven and the other situated in the base of the oven. These ovens are designed to eliminate cold spots and to be used without preheating. The food may, however, take slightly longer to cook.

☐ Halogen heating lamps which facilitate quick browning and easy grilling.

It is up to the individual cook to choose which heat source best suits their needs.

A great variety of dishes can be cooked in the versatile combination oven

The Sanyo 5710 oven

WHICH CYCLE TO USE AND WHEN

One of the most frustrating problems for the microwave/convection owner is knowing what type of food to cook on which cycle.

Many foods, such as fish, fruit, vegetables, rice, confectionery, jams and sauces produce the best results when cooked on a microwave-only cycle.

Foods high in egg whites, such as some sponges, pavlovas and souffles, are best cooked on a convection-only cycle. When they are cooked on microwave or microwave/convection, they rise beautifully while the oven is operating, but tend to drop as soon as the oven stops.

Other foods such as pastries, many cakes and roasts, need the dry heat provided by microwave/convection in order to brown the food. Use the following chart to determine the best cooking method.

Some ovens have an automatic combination cooking cycle. This makes life easier and gives good results. It uses weight to calculate cooking time. Simply select the type of food being cooked and its weight — cooking times, microwave power levels and convectional temperatures are then automatically calculated by the oven, which certainly does make life easy.

Grill/Broil Cycle

Some ovens have a built-in grill or broil cycle, which is used in a similar way to a conventional grill. Most of the ovens that have this cycle preheat automatically. All microwave/convection ovens can be used for grilling. If your oven doesn't have a grill/broil cycle, it is important to preheat the oven to 240°C. It is also important to elevate the food being cooked as high as possible. If your oven doesn't come with a special grilling tray or rack, use the high rack supplied with your oven.

COOKWARE

Microwave Cycle: When cooking on the microwave cycle, use cookware that transmits microwave energy. The microwave oven itself doesn't heat up, however, heat is produced within the food cooked in the oven. Therefore it is important to ensure the cookware used can withstand heat. Suitable containers include: microwave-safe plastics, ovenproof glassware, browning dishes and some pottery or ceramic dishes.

Pottery or ceramic dishes must be glazed on the inside. If the dish is unglazed, moisture is often absorbed into the dish. Microwave energy will then heat up the dish as well as the food, slowing down cooking time. To test whether a particular dish is suitable, place it in your microwave oven with a cup of water. Cook it on high (100%) for 1 minute. If the dish is hot and the water cold, the dish is NOT suitable for microwave use. If the dish is cold and the water hot, it is safe to use.

Microwave-safe glassware can be used to cook many dishes

Browning dishes come in different shapes and sizes, but they have one factor in common. They all have a base coated with a special filament, usually tin oxide, which attracts microwave energy. A microwave oven should not be operated without food or moisture inside to absorb the microwave energy. The only exception to this rule is when using a browning dish.

Place dish in your oven for a specified preheating time on high (100%), put food in the dish; turn food over to sear both sides and then microwave using the time and food setting specified in your recipe. Food cooked in a browning dish usually cooks more quickly than other microwaved food because it cooks by both surface heat and microwave energy. Foods normally pan-fried are best microwaved this way.

A browning dish is essential

MEASURING EQUIPMENT

You will need a nest of cups for measuring dry ingredients (1 cup, ½ cup, ⅓ cup and ¼ cup); a set of spoons (1 tablespoon, 1 teaspoon, ½ teaspoon and ¼ teaspoon); and a transparent graduated measuring jug (1 litre or 250 mL) for measuring liquids. Cup and spoon measures are always level.

Standard metric measures:

4 cups	1 litre (32 fl. oz., 2 pints U.S.A.)
1 cup	250 mL (8 fl. oz., ½ pint U.S.A.)
1 tablespoon	20 mL
1 teaspoon	5 mL

WHICH CYCLE

FOOD	MICROWAVE	MICROWAVE + BROWNING DISH	CONVECTION	GRILL	COMBINATION
Batters			*		
Biscuits	*		*		*
Cakes	*		*		*
Casseroles	*				*
Chinese		*			
Chops		*		*	
Choux pastry			*		
Confectionery	*				
Crumbed food		*			*
Fish	*				
Fried eggs		*			
Jams	*				
Meringues			*		*
Omelettes		*			
Pastry					*
Pavlovas			*		
Poached eggs	*				
Poultry	*				*
Preserves	*				
Reheating	*				
Reheating pastry					*
Rice	*				
Roast meats	*				*
Sauces	*				
Sausages		*		*	
Scrambled eggs	*				
Scones			*		*
Slices	*				*
Souffles			*		
Soups	*				
Sponges	*		*		
Steaks		*		*	
Surface browning		*		*	
Grilled sandwiches		*		*	
Vegetables	*				*
Yeast products e.g. breads			*		*

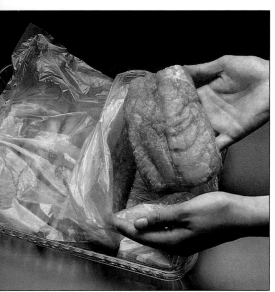

Freezer or oven bags are ideal for steaming and covering food

microwave oven. Some plastic products can break down during microwave cooking. Be careful with plastic wraps, as some of them contain elements which can be absorbed by food during microwave cooking. Plastic wraps made from polyethylene or vinyidene chloride are perfectly safe to use.

Freezer bags and oven bags are ideal for microwave use. Do not, however, use ordinary plastic bags or sandwich bags. When using oven bags do not secure with metal twist ties but use a rubber band or string.

Convection Cycle: When cooking on the convection cycle, traditional metal containers and ovenproof glassware are perfectly safe to use. Some convection-safe plastic cookware is also available. Check manufacturer's guidelines, however, for temperature limits.

Combination Cycle: Metal cake tins and trays can be used on this cycle. If arcing

occurs, place the metal container on a heatproof glass or plate for insulation. Shallow metal containers produce far better results than deep-sided containers. When cooking a deep cake, however, cooking times are increased considerably. It should be remembered when cooking in metal that areas of food covered by the metal container will only cook by convection heat, not by microwave energy. When deep-sided metal containers are used the microwave energy will only cook the top layer.

Ovenproof glass, ceramics, pottery or microwave/convection plastic cookware allow cooking from all sides by both microwave energy and convection heat.

Careful consideration should be given to the type of cookware you choose. Timings differ enormously when using metal containers compared to using glass or plastic. Browning is more successful when you use metal or heatproof glass products rather than plastic.

Foil can be used during the microwave cycle to slow down the cooking process, giving you far greater versatility. Small shallow metal trays are also quite safe provided two basic rules are followed:
☐ Never let metal touch metal — always ensure any foil or metal is elevated if the oven has a metal turntable. The turntable should be able to rotate freely without the metal or foil touching the oven walls.
☐ Always have more food exposed than metal.

Foil can be used to cook a traditional fruit cake without a ring container. Placing a strip of foil around the outside of a fruit cake changes the cooking pattern. Instead of cooking from the outside to the centre, microwave energy is reflected away from the foil, so it enters the food from the top and bottom and cooks evenly through to the centre. Whenever this method of cooking is employed, it is very important to elevate the dish to allow microwaves to enter from top and bottom.

Unevenly shaped pieces of food can be shielded with foil to avoid overcooking, for example with turkey drumsticks or the shank end of a leg of lamb. Foil shielding is also useful on the ends and corners of square or loaf containers.

Small shallow metal trays are very useful for slices and biscuits. Remember the tray must be covered in slice mixture or biscuits and turn freely so it doesn't touch any other metal components in the oven.

With plastic cookware and plastic wraps, only those marked 'suitable for microwave use' should be used in a

Deep Sided Metal Containers

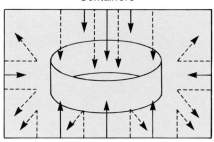

```
---▶  microwaves
——▶  convection heat
```

Microwaves cannot penetrate metal base and sides. Only the top of the cake will cook by microwave. By the time the sides have cooked the top will be overdone. This container is NOT suitable.

Shallow Sided Metal Containers

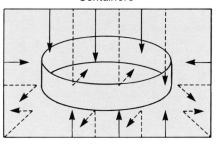

Although the microwaves cannot penetrate sides and base, they will cook well into the cake from the top. This container produces good results.

Ovenproof Glass and Plastic

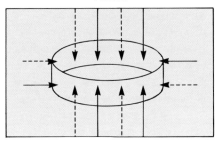

Microwave energy can penetrate from all directions. Cakes cooked in this container produce good results.

MICROWAVE CONVECTION OVENS

BRAND AND MODEL OVEN	NO. COMBINATION SETTINGS	AUTOMATIC COMBINATION	% MICROWAVE	TO	% CONVECTION	VARIABLE TEMPERATURE CONTROL ON COMBINATION	WATTAGE OUTPUT ON MICROWAVE CYCLE
Panasonic Dimension 4 9807	4	Yes	Approx. 36%		64%	Combination 1 140°C Combination 2 150°C Combination 3 160°C Combination 4 190°C	700
Panasonic Dimension 4 9970 or 9870	3	Yes	Approx. Comb. 1 27% Comb. 2 36% Comb. 3 35%		73% 64% 65%	Combination 1 180°C Combination 2 190°C Combination 3 190°C	650
Sanyo 5710	1	No	50%		50%	Yes	680
Sharp Exceller R 8560	2	Yes	High Mix 30% Low Mix 10%		70% 90%	Yes	700
Westinghouse	*	Yes	*		*	*	650
Toshiba ER 961 OA	2	No	High 25% Low 8%		75% 92%	Yes	650

QUICK REFERENCE COOKWARE CHART

TYPE OF COOKWARE	MICROWAVE	CONVECTION	COMBINATION	GRILL
Browning dish	Yes	No	No	No
Microwave only safe plastic	Yes	No	No	No
Microwave/convection plastic	Yes	*Yes	*Yes	No
Ovenproof ceramic and pottery	Yes	Yes	Yes	Yes
Ovenproof glass	Yes	Yes	Yes	Yes
Metal	+ Yes	Yes	Yes	Yes
Foil	+ Yes	Yes	Yes	Yes

*Please check manufacturers' instructions for maximum temperature — DO NOT exceed these temperatures.
+Refer to section on using foil and metal in the microwave

Preheating

Most convection ovens take approximately 10–15 minutes to preheat to 200°C (400°F), depending on the brand. Whether the oven needs to be preheated when using the convection or combination cycles depends on the type of food and how long it takes to cook.

If the food needs to brown and/or crisp the general rule is to preheat the oven if the cooking time is less than 15 minutes. Baked food such as pastries, cakes and scones should always be cooked in a preheated oven. Another rule of thumb: if you would preheat when cooking conventionally, preheat in the microwave combination or convection oven.

When to cover

If you normally cover a particular food when cooking it, you cover it when cooking by microwave or microwave/convection.

When cooking by microwave, plastic wraps may be used. When using the convection cycle, use a lid or cover with foil. Do NOT use plastic wrap. On the combination cycle, it is best to use a lid. If you use plastic wrap it will melt and if you use foil, the top of the food won't cook.

Elevating

With a microwave oven, the middle band has the most even distribution of microwave energy. Therefore most foods cook more evenly if they are elevated. This allows a better flow of microwave energy around the food and cooks evenly from all sides.

With a convection oven, it is usually best to elevate food on a low rack. A high rack will brown the food too quickly. Some ovens come with two racks; the lower rack is used for elevation and the higher rack for grilling.

With a combination oven, elevating on a low rack allows most foods to cook evenly. However, if the food requires considerable browning, it is best elevated on a high rack, especially when using glassware or plastic cookware. If cooking in metal cake tins don't elevate at all, as heat conducted from the metal turntable will help the bottom of the cake to cook.

Cleaning

Microwave ovens are easy to clean and any spills should be wiped up immediately. Clean the walls, oven door, ceiling and turntable thoroughly at least once a week with a damp cloth and a bowl of warm water containing a little dishwashing liquid.

Microwave/convection ovens can be a little more difficult to clean as food can bake onto the oven walls during the convection or combination cycles. Many ovens have an automatic oven cleaner which breaks down any build-up.

All combination ovens have a stainless steel interior. To clean the interior of these ovens, wipe out with detergent and water, then polish if necessary with a stainless steel cleanser. These cleansers will usually remove any stubborn build-up.

Don't let spilt food remain on the turntable. If the turntable is metal or ceramic the food can carbonise and cause damage. Build-up on either the turntable or the oven ceiling can cause arcing and the magnetron may fuse.

Puff or choux pastry can be cooked as successfully in a combination oven as in your conventional gas or electric oven

A NOTE ABOUT OUR RECIPES

All the recipes in this book have symbols:

M   Recipe for ordinary microwave oven or for microwave setting in a microwave/convection oven.

M/C   Recipe for microwave/convection oven.

M or M/C   Recipe for either microwave or microwave/convection cooking.

M and C   Recipe uses both microwave and convection ovens or settings, without using the combination setting available on microwave/convection ovens.

TIMING

The general rule where timing is concerned is to always undercook, remove food from oven, test and, if necessary, replace and cook for a further few seconds or minutes. Nothing tastes worse than overcooked microwaved food and nothing can be done to salvage it, so be warned.

When altering quantities, again the general rule is when you double the quantities, double the cooking time.

When halving quantities, halve the cooking time.

Another important aspect of microwave cooking is standing time. After food has been removed from the oven, it will continue to cook slightly by conduction, that is by the heat still inside the food.

Not all foods require standing time. As a general rule, meats carve more easily and cakes will be less likely to crumble if allowed to stand.

COMBINATION COOKING TIPS

Do not use deep-sided metal cake tins as only the top will cook by microwave energy.

Do not use plastic wraps or paper towel on the combination cycle.

If a metal container causes arcing on the combination cycle insulate the container by sitting it on a heatproof plate.

Always preheat if the cooking time is less than 15 minutes or when cooking pastries and cakes.

To grill, preheat oven to 250°C and elevate on a high rack, the closer the food is to the element, the better the browning achieved.

Elevate on a low rack for an even flow of heat and microwave energy.

Reheat pastry products on the combination cycle.

Cover foods that would normally be covered.

Shallow metal cake tins and slice trays are ideal for combination cooking.

Remember when using metal and foil, always have more food exposed than metal and never have metal touching metal.

Oven bags are ideal for combination cooking. Do NOT use freezer bags on this cycle.

Souffles and pavlovas are best cooked by straight convection.

When using heatproof glass or micro/convection-safe plastic cookware, cooking times are far shorter than when using metal.

Always elevate if cooking in heatproof glass or micro/convection-safe plastic cookware.

Let roast meats stand for 10–15 minutes after cooking for better carving.

Remember always use an oven mit to remove food from the oven.

Anodised cake tins give better results than silver finished cake tins.

Do not let metal tins or trays touch oven walls.

MICROWAVE COOKING TIPS

Always cover food when reheating.

Never use narrow-necked jars.

Always remove foil lids.

Do NOT deep-fry in a microwave oven.

Always remove meat or food from polystyrene containers before defrosting.

Always pierce food that has a membrane i.e. eggs, tomatoes, potatoes etc, so it does not explode.

Always cook for the minimum time, add time as necessary.

Less evaporation occurs in the microwave so you don't need as much liquid in casseroles etc.

Do not grease plastic microwave cookware.

To Toast Coconut
Cook 1 cup of coconut on a plate on high (100%) for 4–6 minutes, stirring after each minute.

To Blanch Vegetables
Cook 2 cups of vegetables in a freezer bag with ¼ cup water, secure end with rubber band. Cook on high (100%) for 2 minutes. Plunge into iced water. Remove water and excess air and freeze.

To Ripen Avocados
Cook firm avocados on medium-low (30%) for 2–3 minutes.

To Open Oysters
Place 6 oysters in shells around turntable, cook on high (100%) for 30 seconds, the shells will pop open.

Chicken
Cook a chicken in an oven bag with a packet of French onion soup or cream of chicken soup for a succulent crisp skinned chicken.

Traditional foods like roasts and terrines can be cooked successfully in a microwave

Take a bought chicken out of the foil-lined paper bag before reheating in the microwave.

Bread
When reheating any bread items, always use paper towel to help absorb excess moisture — never use plastic wraps.

Covering
Whatever is covered when cooking conventionally is usually cooked covered in the microwave.

To Flambe
To flambe your Christmas pudding, heat ⅓ cup favourite spirit in a microwave-proof jug for 30 seconds, ignite and pour over pudding.

Seafood
Cook shellfish in the shell, as microwaves will pass through the shell.

Shellfish high in moisture such as scallops, squid and cuttlefish may 'pop' during cooking. To prevent popping, use a medium (50%) to medium-high (70%) power setting.

Always choose fresh fish that is shiny and firm.

Arrange fish fillets so thicker sections are towards the outside of dish and thinner portions towards the centre for even cooking.

Confectionery
Candy mixtures can reach extremely high temperatures and tend to boil up, so use a large heatproof container.

Chocolate will hold its shape during melting so always stir before adding extra time. It will usually melt during stirring time.

Alcohol affects the setting ability of chocolate if used in excess, so never use more than 2 tablespoons alcohol with 375 g chocolate.

A candy thermometer cannot be used in the microwave. Use a microwave thermometer instead.

Eggs
Pierce the yolk and white when cooking poached or fried eggs.

Eggs will toughen and burst if overcooked. If your eggs are popping, reduce the power setting.

It takes longer to boil an egg in the microwave than on the benchtop, so cook boiled eggs traditionally.

Reheat egg dishes on medium-high (70%).

Sauces
Stir cheese through sauce after cooking.

Ingredients with a high cheese or cream content are best cooked on medium (50%).

Meats
Roast poultry and meats should always be cooked elevated.

Elevate for more even distribution of microwave energy.

If stuffing is added to poultry add an extra 2 minutes cooking time.

An easy way to remember cooking time for poultry, is simply to cook to double the weight — A No. 11 or 1.1 kg chicken would be cooked for 11 minutes on each side or 22 minutes on high (100%).

Popular Poultry Bastes
- ⅔ tomato sauce to ⅓ soy sauce.
- Combined lemon juice and honey.
- Brush with melted butter and sprinkle with paprika.
- Combination of 2 tablespoons soy sauce, 2 tablespoons sherry and finely grated ginger.

Vegetables
Always cook vegetables covered.

Microwaved vegetables retain 90% of their original vitamins and minerals.

Add very little water to vegetables. The more water added the greater the nutrient loss.

RECIPE TESTING

All recipes in this book were prepared and tested by home economists at the Microwave Cuisine Cooking Schools. The author thanks especially the following for their help:
Food preparation: Rachel Blackmore, Lisa Norris, Linda Pearson, Melinda Martin, Sharon Clewer, Ellen French, Tina Gallagher, Karen Pond, Cheryl Charter.

Original typing and help with the manuscript: Belinda Steele.

SNACKS AND STARTERS

Preparing quick snacks, scrumptious first courses or light lunches was never easier than when you use your microwave oven. Select from a variety of pates, soups — chilled for summer, steaming hot for winter — seafood, and delicious savouries perfect for a party platter or a buffet lunch.

Clockwise from top: Garlic Prawns,
Earthy Pea and Ham Soup and
Seafood Pate

Buffet plates Villeroy & Boch   White plates Mikasa and Wedgwood   Cutlery Whitehill

GARLIC PRAWNS

1 kg green (uncooked) king prawns
200 g butter
3 cloves garlic, crushed
1 tablespoon lemon juice
1 tablespoon chopped fresh parsley
sliced chilli rings, to serve

Shell and devein prawns, leaving heads and tails intact. Place butter and garlic in a large microwave-safe casserole dish, then cook on high (100%) for 2 minutes. Add lemon juice, parsley and prawns. Cook covered on medium-high (70%) for 3–5 minutes or until prawns begin to turn pink. Stand covered for 5 minutes. Serve with chilli rings.

Serves 8   M

EARTHY PEA AND HAM SOUP

2 litres hot water
500 g split peas
ham bones
1 small onion, diced
5 peppercorns
1 cup diced ham
1 potato, diced
1 carrot, diced
freshly ground black pepper

Croutons
1 loaf stale white bread
250 g butter, melted

Pastry Top
8 sheets prepared puff pastry
water
1 egg, lightly beaten

Place water, peas, ham bones, onion and peppercorns in a 4 litre microwave-safe casserole dish. Cook, covered, on high (100%) for 25 minutes or until peas are tender, stirring once during cooking. Remove bones. Cut any meat from bones and return it to the soup. Add ham, potato and carrot. Cook, covered, on high (100%) for 15–20 minutes or until vegetables are tender. Sprinkle with black pepper.

To make croutons, preheat oven to 180°C. Remove crusts from bread, cut into 1 cm cubes. Brush each cube with melted butter. Place cubes on two microwave-safe scone trays. Elevate the first tray on a wire rack and place the second tray underneath. Cook until golden.

To cook by micro/convection
Panasonic: Combination 4 for 8 minutes
Sharp: High-Mix 180°C for 8 minutes
Sanyo: Micro/convection 180°C for 8 minutes

Spoon soup into 4 serving dishes with a rim around the edge of each to support pastry. Place a layer of croutons over soup so that they are higher in the centre of the dish than at the sides. Preheat oven to 230°C.

To make pastry top, brush one pastry sheet with water then stack a second sheet on top. Cut to size of serving dish, allowing 2 cm extra all around. Reserve. Roll out remaining pastry on a lightly floured surface and cut into strips 2 cm wide. Place strips around rim of dish, joining any strips with water. Gently place reserved pastry on top and brush with beaten egg. Make a small hole in the centre. Using the back of a knife, decorate pastry by cutting a pattern .25 cm into pastry. Brush top with beaten egg again. Brush pastry rim with water. Gently put top in place and crimp up the pastry edge.

To cook by micro/convection
Panasonic: Combination 4 for 10–14 minutes
Sharp: High-Mix 220°C for 10–12 minutes
Sanyo: Micro/convection 220°C for 10 minutes

Repeat with remaining dishes and serve with extra croutons.

Serves 4   M/C

SEAFOOD PATE

100 g softened butter
1 small onion, finely chopped
12 scallops
500 g white fish fillets, skinned and boned
1 tablespoon chopped fresh parsley
1 clove garlic, crushed
freshly ground black pepper
dash Tabasco sauce
1 tablespoon brandy
½ cup cream
juice ½ lemon
12 king prawns, shelled and deveined
bunch fresh dill
4 shallots

Line a microwave-safe loaf or saddleback dish with greaseproof paper. Grease dish with 50 g butter and chill until set.

Cook 50 g butter and onion on high (100%) for 3 minutes. Add scallops, fish, parsley, garlic, pepper, Tabasco sauce,

brandy, cream and lemon juice. Cook on medium (50%) for 6 minutes, stirring every 2 minutes. Reserve 3 prawns and add remaining prawns to mixture. Cool, place mixture in food processor and process until smooth.

Place half the mixture into the loaf dish. Arrange reserved prawns, half the dill and the shallots lengthways on top of the mixture. Pour over remaining mixture. Chill until set. To serve, remove from container, cut into slices and decorate with remaining dill.

Serves 10   M

CHICKEN CAMEMBERT PARCELS

4 sheets filo pastry
melted butter
4 chicken fillets, skinned
1 Camembert cheese, cut into quarters
freshly ground black pepper

Preheat oven to 230°C. Brush filo pastry with melted butter. Place one chicken fillet, topped with Camembert cheese, in the centre of a pastry sheet. Sprinkle generously with pepper. Fold pastry over to form a parcel. Repeat with remaining chicken fillets. Brush parcels with butter. Place chicken parcels on a greased microwave-safe scone tray. Turn the parcels over halfway through cooking and cook until golden.

To cook by micro/convection
Panasonic: Combination 4 for 15 minutes
Sharp: High-Mix 220°C for 15 minutes
Sanyo: Micro/convection 220°C for 13–15 minutes

Serves 4   M/C

COUNTRY PATE

250 g chicken livers
¼ cup fresh orange juice
1 tablespoon orange Curacao
200 g fresh mushrooms, roughly chopped
1 tablespoon brandy
12 rashers bacon, rinds removed
3 cloves garlic, crushed
2 eggs
¼ cup cream
freshly ground black pepper
½ teaspoon allspice
250 g minced veal
250 g minced pork
300 g minced pork fat
¼ cup flour
watercress, to garnish

Combine chicken livers, orange juice, Curacao, mushrooms and brandy. Marinate 1 hour.

Line a microwave-safe glass loaf container with bacon rashers, so they overlap one another and the ends hang over sides of container.

Drain chicken liver mixture, discarding marinade, and place in blender with garlic, eggs, cream, pepper and allspice and process until smooth. Add chicken liver mixture to veal, pork, pork fat and flour.

Spoon pate mixture into the bacon-lined container and fold overhanging bacon over pate. Invert loaf container in a shallow glass baking dish, leaving loaf container in place. Cook elevated on medium (50%) for 25 minutes or cook by micro/convection (see below).

To cook by micro/convection
Panasonic: Combination 3 for
            45 minutes
Sharp: High-Mix 160°C for
            40 minutes
Sanyo: Micro/convection 160°C
            for 35 minutes

Drain off fat and allow to cool. Turn loaf container upright again, put a weight on top and chill overnight. Remove terrine from loaf container. Cut into slices, garnish with watercress and serve with melba toast or savoury biscuits.

Serves 10   M or M/C

MELBA TOAST

6 slices white bread, crusts removed

Preheat oven to 180°C. Cut bread in half diagonally to make triangles. Place bread triangles on a microwave-safe scone tray. Cook until golden.

To cook by micro/convection
Panasonic: Combination 4 for
            7–10 minutes
Sharp: High-Mix 180°C for
            7–10 minutes
Sanyo: Micro/convection 180°C
            for 6–8 minutes

Makes 12 pieces   M/C

HOT ANCHOVY, CAPER AND GARLIC DIP

2½ cups cream
50 g canned anchovies, drained and
    chopped
4 tablespoons capers, drained
1 clove garlic, crushed
mustard cress, to garnish

Using a microwave-safe jug or dish, cook cream on high (100%) for 18 minutes or until thick, stirring every 5 minutes. Stir in anchovies, capers and garlic. Decorate with mustard cress. Serve with garden fresh vegetables cut into batons.

Serves 8   M

Clockwise from top: Chicken Camembert Parcels, Country Pate, Hot Anchovy, Caper and Garlic Dip and Melba Toast

HAM AND CHEESE CRESCENTS

½ cup milk
40 g butter
2 tablespoons water
1 tablespoon sugar
1 tablespoon dry yeast
1½–2 cups flour
1 teaspoon salt

Filling

½ onion, finely chopped
1 teaspoon butter
200 g ham, minced
1 cup grated cheese
freshly ground black pepper

In a microwave-safe jug combine and warm milk, butter and water together on high (100%) for 1 minute then stir in sugar. Sprinkle yeast over milk mixture, stir and leave until frothy.

Place 1 cup flour and salt in a bowl. Mix in milk mixture and add remaining flour to make a soft dough. Knead by hand for 7–10 minutes. Place dough in a greased bowl, cover with plastic wrap and allow to rise until double in size.

To make filling, cook onion and butter on high (100%) for 1 minute. Mix in ham, cheese and pepper.

Roll dough out into a circle about 25 cm in diameter. Sprinkle filling over dough and cut into eight wedges. Roll each wedge up from the wide end.

Arrange crescents on two greased microwave-safe scone trays, cover them with plastic wrap and allow to rise. Preheat oven to 200°C. Place one tray on a wire elevation rack, the other underneath.

To cook by micro/convection

Panasonic: Combination 4 for 4 minutes then convection 200°C for 8–10 minutes
Sharp: High-Mix 200°C for 4 minutes then convection 200°C for 8–10 minutes
Sanyo: Micro/convection 200°C for 4 minutes then convection 200°C for 8–10 minutes

Remove top tray from oven. Place bottom tray on the rack and cook for a further 3–5 minutes on convection.

Makes 8   M/C

PUMPKIN SOUP

6 x 200–300 g golden nugget pumpkins
1 cup water
20 g butter
1 onion, finely chopped
3 rashers bacon
2 cups milk
1 cup thickened cream
1 teaspoon curry powder
freshly ground black pepper
whipped cream, to decorate
ground nutmeg

Cut top off pumpkins, scoop out seeds and soft centre, and weigh pumpkins. Place a little water inside each pumpkin, replace top, cook elevated on high (100%) for 8–10 minutes per 500 g or until pumpkin flesh is cooked. Drain off liquid and reserve. Cool for 10 minutes, carefully remove flesh leaving a thin layer of flesh in each shell.

Combine flesh and reserved liquid in food processor and process until smooth. Place butter, onion and bacon in a 2 litre microwave-safe dish and cook on high (100%) for 3 minutes. Add milk, cream, curry powder, pepper and pumpkin. Cook on medium-high (70%) for 6 minutes or until hot. Return to food processor and process until smooth. Heat pumpkin shells on high (100%) for 3 minutes, pour soup into shells and decorate with whipped cream and nutmeg.

Serves 6   M

INDIVIDUAL BLUE CHEESE AND SHALLOT QUICHES

25 g butter
3 shallots, finely chopped
3 eggs, lightly beaten
100 g blue cheese, chopped
½ cup sour cream
paprika

Place butter and shallots in a microwave-safe jug and cook on high (100%) for 1½ minutes. Mix in eggs, blue cheese and sour cream. Cook on high (100%) for 2–3 minutes, stirring every 30 seconds, until mixture thickens and resembles scrambled egg.

Pour into four individual quiche dishes and sprinkle with paprika. Cook on medium-high (70%) for 3–4 minutes or until set.

Serves 4   M

CHICKEN AND TUNA TERRINE WITH SOUBISE SAUCE

1 slice wholemeal bread, crusts removed
½ cup milk
375 g chicken breasts, cooked
185 g canned tuna, drained
¼ cup chopped fresh parsley
1 egg, lightly beaten
1 tablespoon capers, rinsed and drained
2 shallots, chopped
1 clove garlic, crushed
juice and rind 1 lemon

Soubise Sauce

1 large onion, sliced
boiling water
20 g butter
1 tablespoon flour
½ cup milk
¼ cup cream
freshly ground black pepper
nutmeg

Soak bread in milk for 5 minutes then squeeze bread dry. Combine bread and milk with remaining terrine ingredients in food processor and process until smooth. Pour mixture into a 2 litre ring mould and cook on medium (50%) for 10 minutes. Drain off any excess liquid, cover with foil and chill overnight.

To make the sauce, cover onion with boiling water, stand for 10 minutes and drain. Cook onion and butter in a microwave-safe dish on high (100%) for 2–3 minutes. Mix in flour, then slowly stir in milk and cream. Cook on high (100%) for 3–4 minutes or until mixture thickens. Stir every minute. Pour sauce into food processor and process until smooth. Heat sauce on high (100%) for 1–2 minutes. Season with pepper and nutmeg.

To serve, cut terrine into slices and serve with warm Soubise Sauce.

Serves 10

Clockwise from top: Ham and Cheese Crescents, Individual Blue Cheese and Shallot Quiche, Pumpkin Soup

21

GRAND MARNIER PATE

500 g chicken livers
180 g butter, softened
1 clove garlic, crushed
6 shallots, chopped
2 tablespoons Grand Marnier
¼ teaspoon nutmeg
freshly ground black pepper
2 tablespoons cream
orange wedges, to garnish

Place chicken livers, butter, garlic, shallots, Grand Marnier, nutmeg and pepper in food processor and process to roughly chop. Cook mixture on high (100%) in a microwave-safe dish for 8 minutes. Allow to cool slightly. Return to food processor, add cream and process until smooth. Spoon mixture into 8 ramekins and chill until set. Serve garnished with thin orange wedges.

Serves 8   M

SCALLOPS IN WINE TOPPED WITH PASTRY HEARTS

Pastry Hearts
2 sheets ready-rolled puff pastry, each 40 cm x 50 cm
1 egg, lightly beaten

Sauteed Scallops
50 g butter
1 clove garlic, crushed
1 teaspoon flour
½ cup white wine
1 teaspoon chopped fresh dill
500 g scallops, cleaned and bearded
1 tablespoon cream
fresh dill, to decorate

Preheat oven to 230°C. Using a heart-shaped pastry cutter, cut 12 pastry hearts. Brush each heart with beaten egg. Place 6 hearts at a time on a greased microwave-safe scone tray and cook elevated until golden brown. Repeat with remaining 6 hearts.

To cook by micro/convection

Panasonic:	Combination 4 for 6 minutes
Sharp:	High-Mix 230°C for 5 minutes
Sanyo:	Micro/convection 240°C for 4 minutes

Remove tray from oven and cool hearts on tray.

Place butter and garlic in a microwave-safe dish. Cook on high (100%) for 30 seconds or until butter melts. Blend flour with a little wine and mix to a paste. Slowly stir in remaining wine. Combine with butter and garlic. Add dill and scallops and stir. Cook on medium (50%) for 6 minutes or until mixture thickens then stir in cream.

To serve, place a pastry heart on each plate and top with filling. Place another pastry heart on top and decorate with dill.

Serves 6   M/C

OYSTERS KILPATRICK

24 oysters in shells
3 teaspoons lemon juice
3 teaspoons Worcestershire sauce
freshly ground black pepper
50 g bacon, finely chopped

Sprinkle oysters with combined lemon juice, Worcestershire sauce, pepper and chopped bacon. Place oysters on a microwave-safe tray and cook elevated on a high wire rack.

To cook by micro/convection
  Panasonic: Combination 3 for
                    4 minutes
  Sharp: High-Mix 180°C for
                    4 minutes
  Sanyo: Micro/convection 180°C
                    for 4 minutes

Serves 4   M/C

OYSTERS BASIL

90 g butter
1 garlic clove, crushed
1 tablespoon chopped fresh basil
1 teaspoon French mustard
1 teaspoon lemon juice
24 oysters in shells
lemon twists, to garnish

Cream together butter, garlic, basil, mustard and lemon juice. Spoon ½ teaspoonful of mixture onto each oyster. Place oysters in the microwave, arranging them in a circle. Cook on medium (50%) for 6 minutes or until mixture melts. Garnish with lemon twists.

Serves 4   M

OYSTERS IN DINNER JACKETS

16 oysters
2 tablespoons French mustard
freshly ground black pepper
8 rashers bacon, rinds removed

Dot each oyster with French mustard, then sprinkle with pepper. Slice bacon rashers in half lengthways. Wrap each mustard-topped oyster in a strip of bacon, securing the end with a toothpick. Place on several sheets of paper towel, then cook on medium-high (70%) for 6 minutes. Serve with pre-dinner drinks.

Makes 16   M

Left to right: Oysters Kilpatrick and Oysters Basil

TOMATO AND AVOCADO TWIN SOUP

Avocado Soup

1 ripe avocado, peeled and seeded
1 tablespoon lemon juice
1 clove garlic, crushed
1¼ cups cream
1 cup milk
freshly ground black pepper

Tomato Soup

1 onion, diced
1 tablespoon oil
1 tablespoon chopped fresh dill
250 g tomato puree
2 cups chicken stock
freshly ground black pepper
mustard cress, to decorate

Place avocado, lemon juice and garlic in food processor, and process until smooth. Pour mixture into a microwave-safe jug. Gently stir in cream, milk and pepper until combined. Heat on medium-high (70%) for 4 minutes, then stir.

Place onion, oil and dill in a microwave-safe jug. Cook on high (100%) for 2 minutes. Mix in remaining tomato soup ingredients. Strain through a fine sieve, to remove onion and dill, into a jug. Heat on medium-high (70%) for 4–8 minutes, stirring once.

To serve, pour both soups slowly into opposite sides of each serving bowl. Decorate with mustard cress.

Serves 4

DEVILLED NUTS

125 g cashew nuts
30 g butter
½ teaspoon dry mustard
½ teaspoon paprika
½ teaspoon cayenne pepper
½ teaspoon celery salt
½ teaspoon salt
1 teaspoon chilli powder

Combine nuts and butter in a microwave-safe bowl and cook on high (100%) for 3 minutes, stirring once during cooking. Turn onto paper towel to cool slightly. Put spices into a freezer bag, add nuts and toss to coat. Serve with pre-dinner drinks.

Makes 1 cup

HOT AVOCADOS WITH WALNUTS AND PECANS

30 g butter, softened
30 g mixed walnuts and pecans, roughly chopped
2 teaspoons lemon juice
freshly ground black pepper
dash cayenne pepper
2 firm avocados, halved and seeded

Combine butter, nuts, lemon juice and peppers. Halve mixture and roll the halves into balls. Wrap in plastic wrap and chill until firm.

Place each ball between two avocado halves. Wrap in plastic wrap and chill until ready to cook. Arrange avocados in a shallow microwave-safe dish and cook on medium (50%) for 3 minutes. Cut walnut and pecan centres in half, thus separating avocado halves.

Serves 4 M

Clockwise from top: Hot Avocados with Walnuts and Pecans, Tomato and Avocado Twin Soup and Spicy Beef Triangles

SPICY BEEF TRIANGLES

1 onion, finely chopped
1 clove garlic, crushed
1 teaspoon butter
2 tomatoes, peeled and roughly chopped
1 teaspoon chopped fresh ginger root
½ small red chilli, finely chopped
1 tablespoon tomato paste
freshly ground black pepper
250 g lean mince
500 g roll prepared puff pastry
1 egg, lightly beaten

In a microwave-safe dish combine and cook onion, garlic and butter on high (100%) for 2 minutes. Add tomatoes, ginger, chilli, tomato paste and pepper. Cook on high (100%) for 5-7 minutes or until tomato sauce has thickened. Add mince, mix well. Cook on high (100%) 7-8 minutes to make a thick mince sauce. Allow to cool.

Preheat oven to 200°C. Cut pastry into 8 cm squares. Place a small spoonful of beef mixture on one half of each square, brush edges with beaten egg. Fold pastry over to form a triangle. Crimp edges with a fork. Brush with beaten egg.

Arrange triangles on two greased microwave-safe scone trays. Place one tray in the oven on a wire elevation rack, the other tray underneath.

To cook by micro/convection

Panasonic:	Combination 4 for 10 minutes, remove top tray, place bottom tray on rack, cook on Combination 4 for 5 minutes
Sharp:	High-Mix 200°C for 10 minutes, remove top tray, place bottom tray on rack, cook on High-Mix 200°C for 5 minutes
Sanyo:	Micro/convection 200°C for 10 minutes, remove top tray, place bottom tray on rack, cook micro/convection 200°C for 5 minutes

Repeat until all pastries are cooked.

Makes 24   M/C

CHICKEN BREADCASES

12 slices bread, crusts removed
20 g butter
1 tablespoon flour
1 cup milk
2 cups finely chopped, cooked chicken
60 g mushrooms, finely sliced
freshly ground black pepper

Cook 6 slices of bread on the turntable, on high (100%) for 30 seconds. Press into a microwave-safe muffin tray. Cook on high (100%) for a further 3-4 minutes or until bread is dry. Remove from tray. Repeat with remaining bread slices.

Melt butter on high (100%) for 30 seconds. Stir in flour, then gradually stir in milk. Cook on high (100%) for 3-4 minutes or until the sauce thickens, stirring once during cooking. Stir in chicken, mushrooms and pepper. Cook on high (100%) for 1-2 minutes. Spoon chicken mixture into breadcases and serve.

Makes 12   M

CHILLED CREAM OF CUCUMBER SOUP

25 g butter
½ onion, diced
3 ½ cups hot chicken stock
1 large cucumber
1 sprig fresh mint
2 tablespoons cornflour
150 mL sour cream
fresh mint, to garnish

In a microwave-safe dish combine and cook butter and onion on high (100%) for 2 minutes. Add stock, cucumber and mint sprig. Cook on high (100%) for 15 minutes. Remove the mint. Pour mixture into a food processor and process until smooth.

Blend cornflour with a little water, mix to a paste and add to soup. Cook on high (100%) for 3-4 minutes or until soup thickens. Cool slightly then stir in sour cream. Chill until ready to serve and garnish with mint.

Serves 4   M

CARROT AND ORANGE SOUP

1 onion, chopped
20 g butter
500 g carrots, peeled and sliced
3 cups chicken stock
1 cup fresh orange juice
freshly ground black pepper

Garnish
unflavoured yoghurt
fresh mint leaves

Place onion and butter in a microwave-safe jug and cook on high (100%) for 2 minutes. Add carrots and cook on high (100%) for 5 minutes. Stir in stock and cook on high (100%) for 15 minutes or until carrots are tender. Place carrot mixture, orange juice and pepper in food processor and process until smooth, chill and serve with a swirl of yoghurt and a mint leaf. Can be served hot or cold.

Serves 4   M

SALMON-FILLED BREADCASES

12 slices white bread, crusts removed
butter

Filling
20 g butter
1 onion, diced
2 tablespoons flour
1 ½ cups milk
210 g canned pink salmon, drained
1 tablespoon lemon juice
1 tablespoon chopped chives
freshly ground black pepper
lemon wedges, dill and parsley, to garnish

Preheat convection oven to 220°C. Flatten bread slightly with a rolling pin. Butter both sides of bread and press into 2 metal microwave/safe muffin trays. Place one tray on an elevation rack in oven and the second tray underneath. Swap position of the trays halfway through cooking. Cook until golden brown.

To cook by micro/convection

Panasonic:	Combination 4 for 15 minutes
Sharp:	High-Mix 200°C for 15 minutes
Sanyo:	Micro/convection 200°C for 12 minutes

In a microwave-safe jug cook butter and onions on high (100%) for 1 minute. Stir in flour then gradually stir in milk. Cook on high (100%) for 2-3 minutes, stirring once during cooking. Add remaining ingredients then cook on high 1½ minutes. Stir. Spoon into breadcases. Decorate with lemon wedges, dill and parsley.

Makes 12   M/C

RICE, PASTA AND SAUCES

You can't beat rice and pasta for nutritious, easy meals. Today's health-conscious cooks are cutting down quantities of animal protein and increasing carbohydrate intake. An additional bonus is that this type of food is quick cooking and fuss-free.

Clockwise: Fettucine Marinara,
Chicken Noodle Rigati and Fried Rice

RICE AND PASTA TIPS FOR SUCCESS

- Always cook uncovered. If cooked covered, rice and pasta tend to boil over.
- Rice and pasta cook by the absorption method so there isn't any real time saving when cooked in the microwave. However the quality of the rice and pasta is to be recommended.
- Rice appears flat when cooked. Fluff up with a fork.

To heat plates, place wet paper towel between each plate and heat on high for 2 minutes or place plates on top of casserole while cooking.

RICE AND PASTA COOKING CHART

FOOD	OTHER INGREDIENTS	COOKING TIME ON HIGH (100%)
1 cup white rice	2 cups cold water	12 minutes
1 cup brown rice	2¼ cups cold water	25–30 minutes
1 cup macaroni	3 cups boiling water 1 tablespoon oil	10–12 minutes
250 g spaghetti	4 cups boiling water 1 tablespoon oil	12–14 minutes

BOILED RICE

1 cup rice
2 cups water

Combine rice and water in a large microwave-safe dish. Cook uncovered on high (100%) for 12 minutes. Fluff up rice with a fork to serve.

Serves 4

FRIED RICE

3 rashers bacon, chopped
1 small onion, diced
30 g mushrooms, diced
2 eggs, lightly beaten
3 cups cooked rice
1 tablespoon soy sauce
2 shallots, chopped
30 g cooked prawns, shelled

Preheat a browning dish on high (100%) for 5 minutes. Add bacon, onion and mushrooms and cook on high for 2 minutes. Fold egg into rice and add to the browning dish. Stir and cook on high (100%) for 2 minutes. Gently stir in soy sauce and cook on high (100%) for 2 minutes. Add shallots and prawns, cook on high (100%) for 2 minutes and serve.

Serves 6

SAVOURY NOODLES

2 litres hot water
250 g noodles
1 teaspoon oil
4 rashers bacon, chopped
½ cup shallots, chopped
1 cup grated cheese
pepper

Place water in a 4 litre microwave-safe casserole dish and cook on high (100%) for 5 minutes or until water boils. Add noodles and oil. Cook on high (100%) for 10 minutes and drain.

Place bacon between pieces of paper towel then cook on high (100%) for 3 minutes. Add bacon and remaining ingredients to noodles and mix thoroughly. Cook on high (100%) for 4½ minutes or until cheese has melted.

Serves 6

FETTUCCINE MARINARA

3 litres hot water
1 tablespoon oil
250 g green fettuccine

Sauce
20 g butter
2 shallots, sliced
1 clove garlic, crushed
1 tablespoon flour
1 cup white wine
½ cup cream
freshly ground black pepper
500 g fresh seafood from fishshop (e.g. squid, prawns, scallops, fish pieces)

Pour water into a 4 litre microwave-safe casserole dish and cook on high (100%) for 10 minutes. Stir in oil and fettuccine, cook on high (100%) for 5 minutes then drain. Fold in a little extra oil and cover while making seafood sauce.

To make the sauce, combine butter, shallots and garlic in a microwave-safe jug. Cook on high (100%) for 2 minutes. Stir in flour, wine, cream and pepper. Cook on medium-high (70%) for 2 minutes or until mixture begins to thicken, stirring after each minute. Gently mix in seafood and cook on medium-high (70%) for 2 minutes. Stir. To serve, spoon seafood sauce over fettuccine.

Serves 4

CHICKEN NOODLE RIGATI

1 tablespoon oil
100 g mushrooms, sliced
1 onion, diced
2 tablespoons flour
2 cups milk
½ capsicum, finely chopped
1 chicken, cooked and boned
freshly ground black pepper
100 g noodles, cooked
2 tablespoons chopped fresh parsley

Place oil, mushrooms and onion in a 2 litre microwave-safe casserole dish and cook on high (100%) for 5 minutes, stirring once. Stir in flour and milk. Add capsicum, chicken, pepper, noodles and half the parsley. Cover and cook on high (100%) for 5–7 minutes or until thickened, stirring every 2 minutes. Serve sprinkled with remaining parsley.

Serves 6

Vegeroni Salad

VEGERONI SALAD

4 cups hot water
5 tablespoons olive oil
250 g vegeroni pasta
½ cup fresh lemon juice
freshly ground black pepper
dash chilli powder
dash dry mustard powder
1 tablespoon finely chopped fresh basil
1 tablespoon finely chopped fresh chives
1 tablespoon finely chopped fresh
  parsley

Cook water and 1 tablespoon oil in a casserole on high (100%) for 5 minutes. Add vegeroni, cook uncovered on high (100%) for 12 minutes. Drain and rinse in cold water. Fold in 1 tablespoon oil.

Combine lemon juice, remaining oil, pepper, chilli powder, mustard and a sprinkle of basil, chives and parsley in a screw top jar. Shake well. Place cooked vegeroni in a salad bowl, sprinkle with remaining fresh herbs and pour dressing over. Toss to coat pasta well with dressing. Chill until ready to serve.

Serves 4–6 ☐M

MACARONI CHEESE

2 cups macaroni
3 cups water
1 onion, finely diced
150 g butter
¼ cup flour
2 cups milk
2½ cups grated cheese
¼ cup chopped fresh parsley

Place macaroni, water, onion and 100 g butter in a 4 litre microwave-safe dish. Cook on high for 12 minutes then drain.

Melt 50 g butter in a microwave-safe jug and cook on high (100%) for 45 seconds. Stir in flour and add a little milk to make a smooth paste. Gradually stir in remaining milk. Cook on high (100%) for 5–6 minutes or until sauce thickens. Add grated cheese (reserving ½ cup), stir until melted. Fold sauce through macaroni mixture. Sprinkle with remaining cheese and chopped parsley.

To cook by micro/convection

Panasonic:	Combination 4 for 12 minutes then on convection 200°C for 5 minutes
Sharp:	Low-Mix 250°C for 10 minutes then 5 minutes on convection at 200°C
Sanyo:	Micro/convection 240°C for 10 minutes then on convection at 200°C for 5 minutes

Serves 6 ☐M/C

CHILLI LASAGNE WITH BECHAMEL SAUCE

1 onion, diced
20 g butter
500 g topside mince
3 large tomatoes, peeled and diced
1 stalk celery, chopped
1 clove garlic, crushed
140 g canned tomato paste
1 tablespoon chilli sauce
pinch fresh thyme, basil and oregano
7–10 prepared lasagne sheets

Bechamel Sauce
25 g butter
3 tablespoons flour
600 mL milk
pinch nutmeg
freshly ground black pepper

Topping
3 cups cheese, grated
paprika (microwave only)

Place onion and butter in a 2 litre microwave-safe casserole dish. Cook on high (100%) for 2 minutes. Add mince, tomatoes, celery, garlic, tomato paste, chilli sauce and herbs. Stir to combine and cook on high (100%) for 5 minutes.

To make sauce, place butter in a microwave-safe jug. Cook on high (100%) for 30–45 seconds or until butter has melted. Stir in flour. Gradually add the milk, nutmeg and pepper. Cook on high (100%) for 5–7 minutes or until sauce has thickened. Stir every 2 minutes.

Dip lasagne sheets in boiling water. In a large greased, microwave-safe glass baking dish, make layers of lasagne, meat mixture, bechamel sauce and grated cheese. Finish with a layer of sauce topped with cheese.

Sprinkle top with paprika, cover and cook on medium (50%) for 10 minutes. Remove cover and cook on high (100%) for 3 minutes. Stand for 5 minutes. Alternatively, cook by micro-convection (see below).

To cook by micro/convection
Preheat oven to 220°C.

Panasonic:	Combination 4 for 35 minutes
Sharp:	High-Mix 220°C for 25 minutes
Sanyo:	Micro/convection 220°C for 25 minutes

Note: To test for doneness, pierce centre of lasagne with a sharp knife. If pasta is soft, lasagne is cooked.

Serves 6–8   M or M/C

BROWN RICE TUNA PIE

Base
2 cups brown rice
4 cups hot water
¼ cup chopped fresh parsley
2 eggs, lightly beaten

Filling
1 cup blanched spinach, drained and chopped
1 cup shallots, chopped
1 red capsicum, chopped
440 g canned tuna, drained and flaked
2 eggs lightly beaten
1 cup unflavoured yoghurt
¾ cup milk
½ cup wheatgerm
freshly ground black pepper
1 cup grated tasty cheese
paprika

Place rice and water in a large microwave-safe casserole dish. Cook uncovered on high (100%) for 30 minutes or until liquid is absorbed. Fluff up with a fork. Fold in parsley and eggs. Press rice mixture firmly into a 25 cm microwave-safe flan dish.

To make filling, spread spinach over rice base and sprinkle with shallots and capsicum. Mix together tuna, eggs, yoghurt, milk, wheatgerm and pepper. Pour the mixture into the flan. Sprinkle with cheese, then paprika.

Elevate and cook on medium-high (70%) for 15 minutes. Shield the sides of the flan dish with foil to prevent overcooking. Cook on medium-high (70%) for 10 minutes. Alternatively, cook by micro/convection (see below).

To cook by micro/convection
Elevate.

Panasonic:	Combination 4 for 20 minutes
Sharp:	High-Mix 180°C for 20 minutes
Sanyo:	Micro/convection 180°C for 15 minutes

Note: To blanch 1 cup spinach, place in a freezer bag, twist end and place under bag. Cook on high (100%) for 1½ minutes. Cut one corner to drain.

Serves 6   M or M/C

SAFFRON RICE RING

2 cups white rice
2 onions, diced
½ teaspoon saffron powder
40 g butter
2½ cups chicken stock
watercress, to garnish

Combine all ingredients in a 2 litre microwave-safe casserole dish. Cook uncovered on high (100%) for 12 minutes. Fluff up with a fork and press into a 20 cm ring container. Decorate with watercress.

Serves 6   M

FETTUCCINE WITH BACON AND MUSHROOM SAUCE

2 litres hot water
1 tablespoon oil
500 g fettuccine

Sauce
250 g bacon, chopped
1 teaspoon butter
4 shallots, chopped
1 cup mushrooms, chopped
2 heaped tablespoons flour
1 cup white wine
1 cup cream

Place water and oil in a 4 litre microwave-safe casserole dish. Cook on high (100%) for 5 minutes, add fettuccine and cook uncovered on high (100%) for 12 minutes then drain.

To make sauce, combine bacon, shallots and butter in a microwave-safe jug. Cook on high (100%) for 4 minutes. Add mushrooms and cook on high (100%) for 1 minute. Stir in flour, and gradually add wine and cream. Cook on high (100%) for 2 minutes. Stir, cook on high (100%) for further 2 minutes or until thickened.

Serves 6   M

Clockwise from top: Brown Rice Tuna Pie, Chilli Lasagne with Bechamel Sauce and Saffron Rice Ring

GREEN HERB SAUCE

1 bunch spinach, washed and chopped
3 tablespoons chopped fresh chervil
1 cup chopped fresh parsley
3 tablespoons chopped chives
3 shallots, chopped
20 g butter
1 tablespoon flour
1 cup milk
freshly ground black pepper
¼ cup cream

Place spinach in freezer bag, cook on high (100%) for 4 minutes then drain. Puree spinach, herbs and shallots.

Using a microwave-safe bowl or jug, melt the butter on high (100%) for 30 seconds, mix in flour, then gradually add milk and cook on high (100%) for 2–3 minutes or until thickened, stirring after each minute.

Carefully mix spinach puree into butter sauce and season with pepper. Heat on medium-high (70%) for 2 minutes stirring after 1 minute. Stir in cream and serve with hot pasta.

Makes 3 cups

TOMATO SAUCE

425 g canned tomatoes in juice
1 onion, finely chopped
2 tablespoons finely chopped fresh basil
freshly ground black pepper
1 cup white wine
1 tablespoon tomato paste

Place all ingredients in a 2 litre microwave-safe jug. Cook on high (100%) for 20–25 minutes or until reduced to a thick tomato sauce. Stir 2 or 3 times during cooking. Serve with hot pasta.

Makes 3 cups

PARSLEY SAUCE

60 g butter
3 tablespoons flour
2 cups milk
freshly ground black pepper
¼ cup finely chopped fresh parsley

In a microwave-safe jug melt butter on high (100%) for 30 seconds. Mix in flour, then a little milk to form a smooth paste. Gradually add remaining milk. Cook on high (100%) for 4–5 minutes or until thickened. Stir after 2 minutes. Season with pepper and stir in parsley.

Makes 2 cups

BOLOGNESE SAUCE

1 onion, diced
20 g butter
500 g lean mince
3 large tomatoes, peeled and roughly chopped
1 stalk celery, sliced
1 clove garlic, crushed
140 g canned tomato paste
1 teaspoon dried thyme
1 teaspoon dried basil
1 teaspoon dried oregano
freshly ground black pepper

In a 2 litre microwave-safe casserole dish, cook onion and butter on high (100%) for 2 minutes. Add remaining ingredients, stir well and cook uncovered on high (100%) for 10 minutes. Stir once during cooking. Serve with hot pasta.

Makes 6 cups

MARSALA SAUCE

3 tablespoons dripping from meat
2 tablespoons flour
1 ¾ cups beef stock
¼ cup Marsala
freshly ground black pepper

Mix dripping with flour, mix a little beef stock to form a smooth paste. Gradually add remaining stock and Marsala. Cook on high (100%) for 4–5 minutes or until thickened, stirring after 2 minutes. Season with pepper and serve.

Makes 2 cups

HERBY CHEESE SAUCE

60 g butter
3 tablespoons flour
1 cup milk
1 cup chicken stock
1 tablespoon finely chopped fresh parsley
1 tablespoon finely chopped fresh chives
½ teaspoon dried rosemary
½ teaspoon dried thyme
½ cup grated tasty cheese
freshly ground black pepper

In a microwave-safe jug melt butter on high (100%) for 30 seconds. Mix in flour, then a little milk to form a smooth paste. Gradually add remaining milk and the stock. Cook on high (100%) for 4–5 minutes or until thickened. Stir after 2 minutes. Stir in herbs and cheese and season with black pepper.

Makes 2 cups

BEARNAISE SAUCE

1 shallot, chopped
¼ cup tarragon vinegar
3 egg yolks
½ cup melted butter
freshly ground black pepper

In a microwave-safe jug cook shallot and vinegar on high (100%) for 1½–2 minutes or until reduced by half. Allow to cool and discard shallot.

Whisk egg yolks and reduced vinegar together. Whisk into melted butter. Cook on medium (50%) for 1½ minutes or until sauce thickens, stirring every 30 seconds. Season with pepper.

Makes 1 cup

HOLLANDAISE SAUCE

3 egg yolks
2 tablespoons lemon juice
½ cup melted butter
freshly ground black pepper

Whisk egg yolks and lemon juice together. Whisk into melted butter. Cook on medium (50%) for 1½ minutes or until sauce thickens, stirring every 30 seconds. Season with pepper.

Makes 1 cup

STIRRED EGG CUSTARD

1 egg
2 tablespoons sugar
1 cup milk, scalded
¼ teaspoon vanilla essence

In a microwave-safe jug whisk egg and sugar. Whisk in milk and vanilla. Cook on medium-low (30%) for 5–7 minutes or until thickened. Stir every 1½ minutes.

Makes 1 cup

Spaghetti served with Tomato Sauce, Green Herb Sauce and Bolognese Sauce

LEMON TUNA SAUCE

1 onion, chopped
1 clove garlic, crushed
1 teaspoon butter
1 tablespoon lemon juice
1 chicken stock cube, crumbled
½ cup water
1 teaspoon French mustard
425 g canned tuna, drained
1 tablespoon cornflour mixed with
*   1 tablespoon cream*
⅓ cup grated cheese
250 g spinach fettucine, cooked

In a microwave-safe jug, cook onion, garlic and butter on high (100%) for 2 minutes. Add lemon juice, crumbled stock cube, water, mustard and tuna. Stir and cook on high (100%) for 1 minute. Add cornflour-cream mixture and cook on high (100%) for 3–4 minutes. Stir in cheese until it melts, pour sauce over hot, cooked pasta and serve.

Serves 4   M

CREAMY SEAFOOD SAUCE

2 hard-boiled eggs
1½ cups milk
1 clove garlic, crushed
1 teaspoon butter
3 tablespoons flour
1 teaspoon dry mustard
freshly ground black pepper
210 g canned smoked mussels or
*   oysters, drained*
3 tablespoons finely chopped fresh
*   chives*
½ cup grated tasty cheese
250 g fettucine, cooked

In a food processor blend eggs and milk until smooth. Cook crushed garlic and butter in a microwave-safe dish on high (100%) for 1 minute. Stir in flour, mustard, pepper and egg-milk mixture and combine well. Cook on high (100%) for 2 minutes, stir in mussels and chives and cook on high (100%) a further 2 minutes. Stir in cheese until it melts, pour sauce over hot, cooked pasta and serve.

Note: prawns, tuna, salmon or any other canned seafood may be substituted for the mussels.

Serves 4   M

THE MAIN EVENT

Whether you serve your main meal at midday or in the evening, this food has to be delicious, filling and nutritious. It helps if it tastes so good you want to share it with friends. The recipes in this section include old favourites like Rack of Lamb, Pepper Steak, Chicken Ballottine, Tournedos and Beef Stroganoff, with new exciting variations to try on your family.

Clockwise from top: Garlic Herbed Chicken, Layered Seafood Slice and Rack of Lamb with Apricot and Almond Stuffing

SEAFOOD TIPS FOR SUCCESS

- Always cover seafood.
- Remove eyes from whole fish before cooking as they will explode.
- Shellfish high in moisture such as scallops, squid and cuttlefish may 'pop' during cooking. To prevent this, use a medium-high (70%) power setting or cook them in a liquid or sauce, e.g. poach in wine or cook in a white sauce.
- Do NOT deep fry fish in the microwave. This is dangerous as there is no way of controlling the temperature.
- Do NOT cook live shellfish in your microwave. Kill lobsters, crabs or crayfish by drowning in fresh water prior to cooking.
- Fish is cooked when the flesh becomes white and will flake easily when tested with a fork.
- Shellfish is cooked when the flesh becomes white. The shells of crustaceans will become pink and gradually turn orange.
- Oysters can easily be opened by placing 6 oyster shells around the turntable or on base of your microwave and cooking on high (100%) for 30 seconds.

SEAFOOD COOKING CHART

FOOD	POWER LEVEL	COOKING TIME PER 500 G
Whole fish	high (100%)	5 minutes
Fillets/cutlets	high (100%)	5 minutes
Prawns, peeled	high (100%)	3–4 minutes
Scallops	medium-high (70%)	4–5 minutes
Mussels	high (100%)	3–4 minutes
Whole green lobsters	high (100%)	10–12 minutes
Whole octopus	high (100%)	8–10 minutes
Squid rings	medium (50%)	4–5 minutes

To help you change recipe quantities should you wish to do so, some recipes in this book give cooking times per 100 g. For example: Cook on high (100%) for 1 minute/100 g.

Remember to read each recipe through and, if necessary, weigh your ingredients before you start cooking.

Left to right: Scallops with Garlic and Coriander Sauce, and Braided Salmon and Perch with Curry Sauce

LAYERED SEAFOOD SLICE

10 large spinach leaves, white removed
500 g white fish fillets
1 slice whole grain bread, crumbed
2 eggs
juice 2 lemons
freshly ground black pepper
220 g canned cooked prawns, drained
150 g uncooked fresh scallops
1 egg white
½ cup cream

Place spinach leaves in a freezer bag. Cook on high (100%) for 2 minutes. Use to line an 18 cm round microwave-safe container, allowing excess to hang over sides. Reserve 1 leaf.

Place fish, breadcrumbs, 1 egg, juice of 1 lemon and pepper in food processor and process until ingredients are well mixed. Spread evenly into spinach-lined dish and press down firmly.

Combine prawns, scallops, remaining egg, egg white, remaining lemon juice and black pepper in food processor. Process until mixed. With motor running add cream then mix until just combined. Spread mixture evenly over first layer. Fold spinach leaves over the mixture, using the reserved leaf to cover completely.

Cook on medium (50%) for 20 minutes, draining twice during cooking. Remove from oven. Place a heavy weight on top and chill overnight. Serve hot or cold cut into thick slices.

Serves 8-10

SCALLOPS WITH GARLIC AND CORIANDER SAUCE

500 g scallops
125 g butter
4 cloves garlic, crushed
freshly ground black pepper
½ cup chopped fresh coriander

Place scallops, butter and garlic in a microwave-safe dish. Cook on medium (50%) for 4 minutes. Stir in pepper and coriander and serve with a green salad.

Serves 4 M

BRAIDED SALMON AND PERCH WITH CURRY SAUCE

1 fillet Atlantic salmon or ocean trout, weighing about 1 kg
1 kg large ocean perch fillets
juice 1 lemon

Curry Sauce
1 small onion, finely sliced
1 tablespoon oil
1 clove garlic, crushed
1 tablespoon mild curry powder
1¼ cups tomato juice
freshly ground black pepper
1 tablespoon lemon juice
2 tablespoons mango chutney
1¼ cups mayonnaise

Remove skin from fish and trim the fillets to 1 cm thick. Cut four 10 cm squares of cardboard and place a square of baking paper on each. Using one cardboard square as a guide, cut 16 strips off each fish to give strips measuring 1 cm × 10 cm. Four strips of each fish will be required to make each braid.

Place four salmon strips lengthways on the cardboard square, making sure that they are equally spaced. Interweave one perch strip through the four salmon strips. Repeat with three remaining perch strips.

With remaining strips make 3 more braids in the same way. Place braids on cardboard in a shallow microwave-safe baking dish, sprinkle with lemon juice and cover. Cook on high (100%) for 6-8 minutes or until cooked.

To make sauce, place onion and oil in a microwave-safe jug. Cook on high (100%) for 1½ minutes. Add garlic and curry powder. Cook on high (100%) for 1½ minutes. Stir in tomato juice, pepper, lemon juice and chutney. Cook on high (100%) for 5 minutes. Strain and reserve liquid. Allow liquid to cool completely then whisk into mayonnaise until smooth. Just before serving, heat on medium-high (70%) for 3-4 minutes, stirring after 2 minutes.

To serve, place some sauce on each plate and slide braid onto plate.

Serves 4

RACK OF LAMB WITH APRICOT AND ALMOND STUFFING

10 prunes, stoned
1 cup sherry
1½ cups soft breadcrumbs
1 small onion, chopped
100 g dried apricots, chopped
⅓ cup almonds, roughly chopped
1 tablespoon chopped fresh parsley
1 egg, beaten
water
2 racks of lamb (6—8 cutlets each)
4 tablespoons redcurrant jelly
1 tablespoon fresh rosemary

Soak prunes in sherry overnight. Drain and set aside. Combine breadcrumbs, onion, apricots, almonds, parsley, egg and sufficient water to moisten. Arrange racks of lamb, interleaving bones, in a microwave-safe dish. Arrange prunes in cavity, then fill with apricot mixture. Coat outside of lamb with jelly and rosemary. Cook on medium-high (70%) for 7 minutes per 500 g of lamb.

Serves 6-8

GARLIC HERBED CHICKEN

100 g butter
1 clove garlic, crushed
2 tablespoons chopped fresh parsley
1 tablespoon chopped fresh chives
freshly ground black pepper
1.2 kg chicken
melted butter

Cream together butter, garlic, parsley, chives and pepper. Using your hand and starting at the neck end of the chicken, separate the skin from the chicken to make pockets. Insert butter mixture into the pockets. Tie the legs of the chicken together and tuck wings under the bird.

Place the chicken on a microwave-safe roasting rack, breast side down and brush with melted butter. Turn over halfway through cooking and brush with more melted butter.

To cook by micro/convection
Panasonic:	Combination 4 for 20 minutes/500g
Sharp:	High-Mix at 200°C for 15 minutes/500 g
Sanyo:	Micro/convection at 200°C for 12 minutes/ 500 g

Serves 4-6 M/C

ROAST POULTRY TIPS FOR SUCCESS

- Food that is compact cooks more evenly, so tuck wings under and tie legs together with an elastic band or string.
- Larger birds, i.e. turkey, may need to have wings and drumsticks shielded with foil to prevent overcooking.
- Always cook elevated on a roasting rack.
- Cook breast side down.
- Cover with baking paper to stop splattering. This will also help to crispen poultry.
- If stuffing the bird you will need to add approximately 2 minutes extra.
- After cooking, cover with foil. This will keep your chicken warm while you prepare the rest of your meal.

Poultry is very low in fat content and won't brown naturally during cooking in the microwave oven. Use a baste to add colour and flavour.

POPULAR BROWNING BASTES

- ⅔ tomato sauce to ⅓ soy sauce.
- Lemon and honey.
- Melted butter and paprika.
- 2 tablespoons soy sauce, 2 tablespoons sherry and 1 teaspoon finely grated fresh ginger.

To Bone A Chicken
Picture 1.
Cut a slit down the back of the bird from the neck to the tail. This will expose the back bone.

Picture 2.
Using a small, sharp knife and keeping the cutting edge against the bone, cut the flesh from the carcass down one side of the bird. Cut through ball joints connecting the wings and legs to the carcass. Continue down the carcass until you reach the ridge of the breast.

Repeat this process on the other side of the bird. Having done this you will be left with the carcass attached to the flesh just at the ridge of the breast bone. Cut bone from carcass very carefully ensuring that skin is not cut or pierced.

Picture 3.
Place the boned chicken skin side down and arrange as above. Cut the wings off at the first joint. Scrape the meat from the bones of the wings and legs. Pull out the bones. The chicken is now ready to use for the ballottine.

POULTRY COOKING CHART

FOOD	POWER LEVEL	COOKING TIME PER 500 G
Whole chicken	high (100%)	10 minutes
Chicken pieces	high (100%)	10 minutes
Turkey	high (100%) then medium-high (70%)	10 minutes 10 minutes
Quail	high (100%)	8 minutes
Duck	high (100%)	10 minutes
Goose	medium-high (70%)	12 minutes

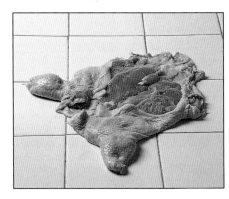

CHICKEN BALLOTTINE

1.5 kg chicken, boned
2 tablespoons soy sauce
2 tablespoons tomato sauce

Stuffing
2 cups shredded spinach
125 g mushrooms, chopped
1 cup fresh breadcrumbs
1 egg, lightly beaten
1 cup grated cheese
2 teaspoons chopped fresh basil
freshly ground black pepper

To make stuffing, cook spinach and mushrooms on high (100%) for 2 minutes. Add remaining stuffing ingredients and mix to combine. Insert stuffing in the centre of the chicken, and arrange the skin around the stuffing to enclose it completely. Sew chicken up using a trussing needle and string and tie string around chicken to give a good shape.

Place chicken, stitched side up, on a microwave-safe roasting rack. Mix soy and tomato sauces together and brush over chicken. Cook on high (100%) for 10 minutes, turn and brush with remaining baste. Cook on high (100%) for 12 minutes. Cover with foil and stand for 10 minutes. Remove all string. To serve, cut into slices.

Serves 6   M

Remove oven odours by combining juice and peel of 1 lemon with water in a bowl, cook on high (100%), for 5 minutes then wipe clean with a damp cloth.

Chicken Ballottine

Plate Royal Copenhagen

Swiss Chicken

PINK AND GREEN PEPPERCORN CHICKEN

60 g packet salt-reduced Cream of
   Chicken soup
³/₄ cup water
1 cup white wine
1 ½ tablespoons pink and green
   peppercorns
¼ cup thickened cream
1.5 kg chicken, cooked, boned and cut
   into pieces

Place soup, water and wine in a 3 litre microwave-safe casserole dish. Cook on high (100%) for 5–6 minutes or until mixture boils and thickens. Stir once during cooking. Stir in peppercorns and cream. Add chicken and stir. Cook on medium (50%) for 3 minutes and serve.

Serves 4

TUNA AND SPINACH BILLABONGS

10 spinach leaves, white removed
1 cup mashed potato
1 onion, chopped
2 tablespoons chopped fresh parsley
1 teaspoon lemon juice
250 g canned tuna, drained

Sauce
40 g butter
¼ cup flour
black pepper
1 teaspoon lemon juice
300 mL sour cream

Put spinach leaves in a freezer bag and cook on high (100%) for 2 minutes. Combine potato, onion, parsley, lemon juice and tuna. Cut each spinach leaf in half and spoon a small amount of mixture on each leaf. Fold sides over, roll up and arrange spinach rolls in a microwave-safe dish.

   To make sauce, place butter in a microwave-safe jug. Cook on high (100%) for 30 seconds or until melted. Stir in flour, add remaining ingredients and cook on medium-high (70%) for 3 minutes or until sauce begins to thicken, stirring once. Pour sauce over spinach rolls and cook on high (100%) for 2 minutes.

Makes 10

WHOLE GINGER SOLE

1 large whole sole, cleaned and scaled
2 tablespoons lemon juice
fresh ginger root, cut into thin strips
dash paprika
1 tablespoon chopped fresh parsley

Place fish on a large shallow microwave-safe dish. Sprinkle lemon juice, ginger, paprika and parsley over the fish. Cover with plastic wrap and cook on high (100%) for 1 minute/100 g.

Serves 2

SWISS CHICKEN

6 chicken breasts, boned and skinned
3 slices ham
6 thin slices Swiss cheese
1 cup dry breadcrumbs
2 tablespoons Parmesan cheese
1 clove garlic, crushed
¼ teaspoon dried tarragon
¼ cup flour
1 egg, lightly beaten
40 g butter
watercress, to garnish

Pound chicken breasts until very thin. Place half a slice of ham and a slice of Swiss cheese on each chicken breast. Roll up and secure with toothpicks. Mix breadcrumbs, Parmesan cheese, garlic and tarragon together. Cover chicken rolls in flour, dip them in egg, then roll in breadcrumbs mixture. Preheat a 25 cm browning dish on high (100%) for 7 minutes. Add butter, swirl to coat dish. Place chicken rolls in hot browning dish, turn over to sear both sides. Cook on high (100%) for 4 minutes or until cooked.

   To serve, place one chicken roll on each plate and decorate with watercress.

Serves 6 M

Plate Royal Doulton

Spinach-filled Chicken with Mousseline Sauce

SPINACH-FILLED CHICKEN WITH MOUSSELINE SAUCE

6 chicken breast fillets
1 shallot, chopped
sprig fresh thyme
wine
1 bunch of spinach, washed, white stalks removed
2 tablespoons cream
freshly ground black pepper
dash nutmeg
6 slices thin leg ham
fresh sage leaves and triangles of red capsicum, to garnish

Mousseline Sauce
3 egg yolks
2 tablespoons lemon juice
1/2 cup melted butter
3 tablespoons lightly whipped cream

Place chicken, shallot and thyme in a large shallow dish and pour wine over to cover. Cover with lid and cook on high (100%) for 10 minutes.

Cook spinach in freezer bag on high (100%) for 5 minutes. Cool, then squeeze spinach as dry as possible. Puree spinach with cream, pepper and nutmeg.

Remove chicken from poaching liquid and place uneven side up. Spread a layer of spinach puree over the chicken and wrap in a slice of ham. Return to dish, cover and cook on medium-high (70%) for 6–8 minutes.

To make the sauce, whisk egg yolks and lemon juice together in a small jug. Whisk egg mixture into melted butter. Cook on medium (50%) for 1 1/2 minutes or until sauce thickens. Stir every 30 seconds. Fold in cream.

To serve, coat each chicken parcel with sauce and garnish with 2 small sage leaves and 2 capsicum triangles.

Serves 6   M

ORANGE CHICKEN DRUMSTICKS

1/2 cup orange juice
3/4 cup pineapple juice
1/2 teaspoon dry mustard powder
1 teaspoon curry powder
3 teaspoons soy sauce
1 chicken stock cube
8 chicken drumsticks
1 tablespoon cornflour

Combine juices, mustard, curry, soy sauce and stock cube, cook on high (100%) for 2 minutes. Pour over drumsticks and marinate several hours or overnight.

Drain drumsticks, reserving marinade and place on a roasting rack. Mix cornflour with a little marinade and cook on high (100%) for 3–4 minutes, stirring once. Baste drumsticks with half the mixture, cook on high (100%) for 10 minutes, turn chicken over and baste with remaining sauce. Cook on high (100%) for 8–10 minutes or until cooked.

Serves 4   M

41

ROAST MEATS TIPS FOR SUCCESS

- Always cook ELEVATED on a roasting rack.
- Cook uncovered or use baking paper or a splatter cover.
- Do NOT cover with plastic wrap or a lid unless cooking by sensor.
- Do NOT add salt as this will toughen the surface of meat (the one exception to this rule is when cooking pork crackling).
- Shield any thinner parts of your roast with foil to avoid overcooking.
- Less tender cuts of meat should be cooked for longer on a lower power setting i.e. MEDIUM–LOW–DEFROST.
- Larger cuts of red meat brown naturally and do not need any browning agents.
- Smaller cuts of meat i.e. chops, steaks, etc. should be cooked in a browning dish or have browning agents added.
- Pot roasts cook perfectly in oven bags.
- Turn large cuts of meat over half way through cooking.
- Always test meat when cooked.
- Cover with foil when cooked to keep warm while you prepare the rest of your meal.

Left to right: Coeur de Filet Wellington, and Rainbow Fillet of Beef

MEAT COOKING CHART

FOOD	POWER LEVEL	COOKING TIME PER 500 G
Beef		
Well-done	high (100%) then medium-high (70%–90%)	10 minutes 10 minutes
Medium	medium-high (70–90%)	9 minutes
Rare	medium (50–70%)	10 minutes
Lamb	high (100%) then medium-high (70–90%)	10 minutes 10 minutes
Pork	high (100%) then medium-high (70–90%)	10 minutes 14 minutes

COEUR DE FILET WELLINGTON

1 kg piece of scotch fillet beef
butter
40 cm × 50 cm piece prepared puff pastry
200 g pate
6–8 mushrooms, sliced
1 egg yolk, lightly beaten

Preheat a 25 cm browning dish on high (100%) for 8 minutes. Place a small amount of butter in browning dish and swirl to coat. Add beef and cook on high (100%) for 2–3 minutes. Remove beef, drain juices from dish and reserve. Reheat browning dish on high (100%) for 4 minutes, add a little more butter and swirl to coat. Add beef, cooked side up. Cook on high (100%) for 2–3 minutes.

Preheat oven to 220°C. Cut off a length of pastry that will wrap around the fillet. Cover beef with pate and mushrooms. Place fillet on pastry sheet, fold ends over fillet, then bring up sides. Join pastry by brushing with egg yolk. Make pastry leaves to decorate the top. Brush generously with egg. Cook until golden brown.

To cook by micro/convection
Panasonic: Combination 4 for 15–20 minutes
Sharp: High-Mix at 200°C for 15–20 minutes
Sanyo: Micro/convection at 200°C for 15–20 minutes or until golden brown.

Serves 6

M/C

Plates Wedgwood   Cutlery Oneida   Glassware Dansao

RAINBOW FILLET OF BEEF

1 kg piece scotch fillet beef
butter
500 g spinach, washed and chopped
½ teaspoon ground nutmeg
freshly ground black pepper
3 rashers bacon, chopped
200 g mushrooms, sliced
2 tablespoons cornflour
2 tablespoons water
2 tablespoons sherry
40 cm × 50 cm piece prepared puff
   pastry
1 egg yolk, lightly beaten

Preheat a 25 cm browning dish on high (100%) for 8 minutes. Place 1 teaspoon of butter in the dish and swirl to coat. Add beef to browning dish and cook on high (100%) for 5 minutes. Remove beef and drain juices. Reheat browning dish on high (100%) for 4 minutes then add another teaspoon of butter. Swirl to coat the dish. Add beef, cooked side up and cook on high (100%) for 5 minutes. Set beef aside to cool.

Cook spinach in a freezer bag on high (100%) for 2–3 minutes. Squeeze spinach dry. Mix together spinach, nutmeg and pepper. Set aside.

In a microwave-safe dish, cook bacon on high (100%) for 2–3 minutes. Add mushrooms and microwave on high (100%) for 2–3 minutes. Mix in cornflour, then water and sherry. Microwave on high (100%) for 1 minute. Stir well and set aside to cool.

Preheat oven to 220°C. Cut two horizontal pockets in beef. Stuff one pocket with the spinach mixture and the other pocket with the mushroom mixture. Place stuffed fillet on pastry. Fold ends of pastry over fillet then bring up sides. Join pastry by brushing each surface with egg yolk, then crimping. Cut pastry leaves from any leftover pastry to decorate. Brush pastry with egg yolk and place in a micro/convection-safe baking dish. Cook until pastry is puffed and golden brown.

To cook by micro/convection
Panasonic: Combination 4 for
             15–20 minutes
Sharp: High-Mix 200°C for
             15–20 minutes
Sanyo: Micro/convection 200°C
             for 15–20 minutes

Serves 6   M/C

Steak and Mushroom Pie with Glazed Meatloaf

GLAZED MEAT LOAF

450 g canned sliced pineapple, drained
750 g topside mince
250 g sausage mince
1 large onion, chopped
1 cup fresh breadcrumbs, firmly packed
2 tablespoons chopped fresh parsley
¾ level teaspoon salt
¾ level teaspoon pepper
1 tablespoon Worcestershire sauce
1 level teaspoon mustard
1 tablespoon tomato sauce
50 g egg, lightly beaten
⅔ cup evaporated milk

Glaze
⅓ cup brown sugar
⅓ cup tomato sauce
cherries, to garnish

Grease a 25 cm × 10 cm × 8 cm microwave-safe loaf dish. Arrange sliced pineapple attractively around base and sides. Combine topside and sausage minces with remaining ingredients, mix well and pack firmly into prepared mould.

Upturn loaf into a microwave-safe baking dish but do not remove loaf dish. Cook on high (100%) for 8 minutes, drain off excess fat and liquid and return to oven in the same way. Cook on high (100%) for a further 8 minutes, drain off remaining liquid then remove loaf dish.

Combine glaze ingredients and pour half over the loaf. Cook on high (100%) for 2 minutes. Pour over remaining glaze then cook on high (100%) for 2 minutes. Arrange cherries over pineapple. Serve hot or cold.

Serves 8   M

STEAK AND MUSHROOM PIE

1 kg blade steak, diced
3 tablespoons flour
16 mushrooms, sliced
4 onions, diced
1 clove garlic, crushed
4 tablespoons chilli sauce
3½ cups beef stock
30 cm × 25 cm piece prepared puff
*   pastry*
1 egg, lightly beaten

Toss steak in flour to coat. Place all ingredients except pastry and egg in micro/convection-safe dish and cover.

To cook by micro/convection
   Panasonic: Combination 3 for 1 hour
   Sharp: High-Mix 160°C for 1
                 hour
   Sanyo: Micro/convection 160°C
                 for 45 minutes

Preheat convection oven to 220°C. Roll out pastry to fit a deep 20 cm microwave-safe pie dish. Cut a strip of pastry to fit around rim of dish. Cut another pastry piece to cover top of dish, allowing for 1 cm overhang.

Add meat to pie dish. Place pastry strip on dish rim, joining any edges with egg. Brush with beaten egg. Add pastry top and trim edges. Make 3 slits. Cut a pastry shape from left-over pastry to decorate the pie. Brush with egg and cook on high (100%) for 2 minutes. Cook on convection 200°C for 12–15 minutes or until pastry is golden.
Note: To coat meat with flour, place meat and flour in a freezer bag, hold top and shake.

Serves 6   M/C

WHISKY TOURNEDOS ON CROUTONS

4 slices bread, about 1 cm thick
4 rashers bacon, rinds removed
4 scotch fillet steaks (2 cm thick)
40 g butter
1 onion, diced
2 cloves garlic
freshly ground black pepper
3 tablespoons whisky
½ cup cream

Cut bread into rounds the same size as steaks. Butter both sides. Preheat a 25 cm browning dish on high (100%) for 4 minutes, add croutons, cook on high (100%) for 1½ minutes, turning over after 45 seconds. Place on paper towel and set aside.

Wrap 1 rasher of bacon around each piece of steak and secure with a toothpick. Preheat a 25 cm browning dish on high (100%) for 8 minutes. Add butter, swirl to coat then add onion, garlic and pepper and cook on high (100%) for 1 minute. Add steaks, cook on high (100%) for 4 minutes, turning halfway through cooking time. Remove meat and cover with foil.

In a microwave-safe jug combine whisky with juices from meat. Stir in cream and cook on high (100%) for 5–6 minutes or until thickened. To serve, place a steak on each crouton and spoon over sauce.
Note: Tournedos are traditionally served rare. For those who prefer their meat well done, cook for an extra 3 minutes.

Serves 4   M

BEEF STRIPS IN CREAM SAUCE

500 g topside steak, cut into thin strips
2 tablespoons flour
1 onion, diced
100 g mushrooms, sliced
2 tablespoons tomato paste
1 capsicum, sliced
2 cloves garlic, crushed
1 cup water
¾ cup red wine
1 tablespoon Worcestershire sauce
½ cup cream

Toss meat in flour. Place all ingredients except cream in a 2 litre micro/convection-safe dish and stir well. Cover and cook on high (100%) for 10 minutes, then on medium (50%) for 25 minutes. Alternatively, cook by micro/convection (see below).

To cook by micro/convection
   Panasonic: Combination 3 for
                 30 minutes
   Sharp: High-Mix 160°C for
                 30 minutes
   Sanyo: Micro/convection 160°C
                 for 30 minutes

Just before serving, stir in cream.

Serves 4   M   or   M/C

PARCELLED PISTACHIO STEAKS

4 steaks, rump or veal
2 slices leg ham
4 slices of Edam cheese
freshly ground black pepper
seasoned flour
2 eggs, lightly beaten
250 g pistachio nuts, peeled and
*   chopped*
1 teaspoon butter

Pound steaks with meat mallet. Place a slice of ham and 2 slices cheese onto each of 2 steaks and sprinkle with black pepper. Top with remaining steaks then cut each parcel in half. Press edges of steaks together. Coat with flour, brush with egg then coat with chopped nuts.

Preheat a 25 cm browning dish on high (100%) for 8 minutes. Add butter and swirl to coat dish. Add steak and turn to sear. Cook on high (100%) for 10 minutes, turning halfway through cooking. Place cooked meat in conventional oven, set on low to keep warm. Serve with garden fresh vegetables.

Serves 4

PEPPER STEAK WITH PINK AND GREEN PEPPERCORNS

5–6 tablespoons cracked peppercorns
4 × 175 g fillet steaks
20 g butter
1 tablespoon oil
2 tablespoons brandy
200 mL thickened cream
1 tablespoon each of pink and green
*   peppercorns*

Preheat a large browning casserole dish on high (100%) for 8 minutes. Press both sides of steak with cracked pepper. Add butter and oil to preheated browning dish, swirl to coat and add steaks. Microwave on high (100%) for 5–6 minutes, turn over, cook on high (100%) for 2–3 minutes or until cooked to your liking. Transfer meat to a warm serving plate.

Stir brandy and cream into remaining juices. Cook on high (100%) for 2–3 minutes till sauce thickens, stirring each minute. Add pink and green peppercorns, pour over steaks and serve immediately.
Note: Peppercorns can be cracked at home by using the food processor.

Serves 4

Clockwise from top left: Steak with
Pink and Green Peppercorns,
Parcelled Pistachio Steaks and
Whiskey Tournedos on Croutons

Garlic Kiwi Lamb

LAMB ROULADE NOISETTES

12 lamb loin chops, boned
12 rashers bacon, rind removed
flour
2 eggs
fine dry breadcrumbs
20 g butter, melted
12 rings pineapple

Roulade Sauce

125 g button mushrooms
½ cup shallots, chopped
20 g butter
140 g canned tomato paste
½ cup white wine
freshly ground black pepper
½ cup cream

Trim each chop into a circle. Wrap bacon around each chop and secure with string. Dip chops into flour then egg then breadcrumbs. Brush with melted butter. Heat browning dish on high (100%) for 8 minutes and add 6 chops. Turn to sear. Cook for 3–4 minutes on each side or until browned. Repeat with remaining chops. Remove string.

To make the sauce, in a microwave-safe dish cook mushrooms, shallots and butter on high (100%) for 2 minutes. Add tomato paste, wine and pepper. Cook on high (100%) for 2 minutes then stir. Cook a further 5 minutes. Stir in the cream.

To serve, sit lamb noisettes on pineapple rings and pour sauce over.

Serves 12   M

GARLIC KIWI LAMB

1 × 8 chop loin of lamb, trimmed and
  boned
black pepper
2 kiwi fruit, peeled
1 clove garlic, crushed
1 tablespoon soy sauce
2 tablespoons honey
1 teaspoon sherry (optional)

Sauce

reserved marinade
water
1 tablespoon cornflour

Flatten out lamb and sprinkle with pepper. Cover with a layer of thinly sliced kiwi fruit using just one of the two fruits. Roll and tie with string. In a microwave-safe dish mash the other kiwi fruit with garlic, soy sauce, honey and sherry. Cook on medium-high (70%) for 1 minute. Pour over lamb and marinate for 1 hour.

Drain meat, reserving marinade and place in an oven bag. Cook on medium-high (70%) for 6–8 minutes. Drain off any liquid. Cook on medium-high (70%) for a further 6–8 minutes. Stand for 10 minutes.

To make sauce, strain marinade and make up to 1 cup with water. Mix cornflour with a little water and stir into marinade. Cook on high (100%) for 45 seconds, stir and cook a further 1 minute or until sauce thickens. Serve with lamb.

Serves 4   M

CORNED SILVERSIDE

1.5 kg piece corned silverside
2 tablespoons brown sugar
2 tablespoons malt vinegar
4–5 cloves
8–9 whole allspice
6 peppercorns
warm water to cover

To calculate the cooking time, allow 26 minutes per 500 g of meat. Rinse meat under cold water or soak for 30 minutes to remove excess salt. Place meat in a 4 litre microwave-safe casserole dish then add remaining ingredients and cover. Cook on high (100%) for 10 minutes, then for the calculated time on medium-low (30%). Allow to stand 10–15 minutes before carving.
Note: Pickled pork can also be cooked using this recipe.

Serves 6 · M

CRUSTY HERBED LEG OF LAMB

1.5 kg–2 kg leg of lamb
2 cloves garlic, crushed
6 tablespoons chopped fresh parsley
2 tablespoons chopped fresh chives
6 tablespoons soft breadcrumbs
125 g butter, softened
juice 1 lemon

Gravy
2 tablespoons flour
2 cups stock
freshly ground black pepper

Elevate leg of lamb in a micro/convection-safe baking dish. Combine garlic, parsley, chives, breadcrumbs, butter and lemon juice. Spread over lamb halfway through cooking. Cook on a low rack.

To cook by micro/convection

Panasonic:	Combination 3 allowing 20 minutes/500 g
Sharp:	High-Mix 180°C allowing 20 minutes/500 g
Sanyo:	Micro/convection 180°C allowing 15 minutes/500 g

Remove from oven, cover with foil and stand for 15 minutes before carving.

To make gravy, drain meat juices into a microwave-safe jug. Stand jug in cold water until juices have cooled then skim fat and discard. Mix remaining juices with flour. Gradually stir in stock and season with pepper. Cook on high (100%) for 5–7 minutes or until gravy thickens, stirring every 2 minutes. Serve gravy over carved lamb.

Serves 6–8 · M/C

TASMANIAN SCALLOPS SAUTEED IN WINE

50 g butter
1 clove garlic, crushed
½ teaspoon chopped fresh basil
500 g scallops, deveined
3 tablespoons white wine

Place butter and garlic in a microwave-safe dish. Cook on high (100%) for 30 seconds or until butter melts. Add basil, scallops and wine then stir. Cook on medium (50%) for 4 minutes and serve.

Serves 4 · M

Crusty Herbed Leg of Lamb

Table linen Jaan China Villeroy & Boch

TERRINE OF HAM, PORK AND VEAL WITH MUSTARD SAUCE

500 g leg ham, finely chopped
500 g pork mince
500 g veal mince
1 clove garlic, crushed
freshly ground black pepper
selection of finely chopped fresh herbs
(thyme, sage or rosemary)
¼ teaspoon nutmeg
½ cup white wine
2 tablespoons brandy
3 rashers bacon, cut into 5 cm strips
2 bay leaves, crumbled

Mustard Sauce
4 eggs, beaten
½ cup brown sugar
½ cup maple syrup
1 cup cider vinegar
¼ cup mustard powder
1 tablespoon flour
cardamom, cloves

Mix together ham, minces, garlic, pepper, herbs and nutmeg. Pour over wine and brandy and marinate for 2–3 hours.

Place half the bacon strips into the bottom of a micro/convection-safe 2 litre ring mould or loaf container. Press in meat mixture. Mix together remaining bacon strips and crumbled bay leaves and sprinkle over top of meat. Invert dish into a shallow micro/convection-safe baking dish, to allow fat to drain off during cooking. Cook elevated on medium (50%) for 20 minutes. Alternatively, cook by micro/convection (see below).

To cook by micro/convection

Panasonic:	Combination 3 for 45 minutes
Sharp:	High-Mix 160°C for 40 minutes
Sanyo:	Micro/convection 160°C for 35 minutes

Drain off fat and cool. Turn meat back into container and place a weight on top. Refrigerate overnight.

Place all sauce ingredients in a 1 litre microwave-safe jug. Mix well and cook on medium-high (70%) for 6 minutes or until mixture thickens, stirring every 2 minutes. Allow to cool. To serve, cut terrine into slices and accompany with mustard sauce.

Serves 10   [M] or [M/C]

Terrine of Ham, Pork and Veal with Mustard Sauce

BEEF STROGANOFF

2 tablespoons oil
1 small onion, diced
1 kg topside or rump steak, cut into thin strips
2 tablespoons tomato sauce
100 g mushrooms, sliced
1 tablespoon cornflour
½ cup water
½ cup sour cream
fresh parsley, to garnish

Preheat a 25 cm browning dish on high (100%) for 8 minutes. Add oil and onion, toss. Add meat and stir to sear. Cook on high (100%) for 5 minutes, stirring after 2½ minutes. Add tomato sauce and mushrooms. Cover and cook on high (100%) for 8 minutes.

Combine cornflour and a little water to form a paste. Stir in remaining water. Add to meat, stirring well. Cook covered on high (100%) for 2 minutes. Just before serving stir in sour cream and garnish with parsley.

Serves 6   [M]

SHEPHERD'S PIE

1 onion, chopped
2 tomatoes, peeled
500 g lean leg lamb, minced
1 green capsicum, cut into strips
1 tablespoon chopped fresh parsley
1 tablespoon finely chopped fresh rosemary
1 tablespoon soy sauce
2 tablespoons flour
¼ cup water

Topping
2 shallots, finely chopped
2 cups mashed potato
50 g butter, melted

Place onion and tomatoes in a microwave-safe jug and cook on high (100%) for 5 minutes. Add lamb, capsicum, herbs and soy sauce, stirring to combine. Cook uncovered on high (100%) for 8 minutes. Stir twice during cooking. Mix flour with water, stir into mixture and cook on high (100%) for 4–5 minutes or until thickened.

Transfer mixture to a 20 cm pie dish. To make topping, combine shallots and potato. Spread mixture over mince and brush with melted butter. Elevate on a low rack and cook until golden brown on the top.

To cook by micro/convection

Panasonic:	Combination 4 for 15 minutes then on convection 240°C for 10 minutes
Sharp:	High-Mix 230°C for 20 minutes
Sanyo:	Micro/convection 240°C for 20 minutes

Note: To cook mashed potatoes in the microwave, wash potatoes and cook them in their skins, allowing 10 minutes per 500 g. Peel skins from the potatoes and mash.

Serves 4–6   [M/C]

SOLE AND SALMON

500 g fresh sole fillets
1 cup chopped fresh parsley, to garnish

Salmon Filling
1 onion, chopped
1 stalk celery, chopped
40 g butter
220 g canned salmon, drained and boned
¼ cup fresh breadcrumbs
freshly ground black pepper

Sauce
40 g butter
1½ tablespoons flour
freshly ground black pepper
1 tablespoon tomato sauce
½ cup cream
¼ cup milk
¼ cup white wine

Place onions, celery and butter in a microwave-safe jug. Cook on high (100%) for 2–4 minutes or until tender. Stir in salmon, breadcrumbs and black pepper. Line the bottom of a microwave-safe loaf container with half the sole fillets. Top with filling mixture and then with remaining sole fillets. Cover and cook on high (100%) for 5–7 minutes or until fish is just cooked.

To make sauce, heat butter in a microwave-safe jug on high (100%) for 30–45 seconds. Stir in remaining ingredients and cook on high (100%) for 3–5 minutes or until sauce is thickened, stirring halfway through cooking.

To serve, turn fish out onto a serving platter and spoon sauce over. Garnish with chopped parsley.

Serves 6   [M]

MEDALLIONS OF PORK WITH GINGER SAUCE

4 pork medallion steaks
1 clove garlic, crushed
1 tablespoon sesame oil

Sauce
1 tablespoon soy sauce
¼ cup honey
1 teaspoon grated fresh ginger root
½ cup orange juice
2 tablespoons cornflour

Trim steaks into neat shapes. Combine garlic and sesame oil and brush over steaks. Preheat a 25 cm browning dish on high (100%) for 8 minutes. Add steaks, cook on high (100%) for 5 minutes, turn over halfway through cooking.

In a microwave-safe jug combine all sauce ingredients except cornflour, cook on high (100%) for 1 minute. Mix a little of this hot mixture with the cornflour, then stir into sauce. Cook on high (100%) for 1 minute or until sauce is slightly thickened. Serve a little sauce with each pork steak.

Serves 4 M

GRAND MARNIER PORK WITH CRACKLING PUFFS

2 kg loin of pork, boned, rind removed and reserved
salt
orange twists, to garnish

Stuffing
250 g spinach leaves, chopped
30 g butter
3 tablespoons pine nuts

Sauce
1 cup water
1 chicken stock cube
1 tablespoon vinegar
1 tablespoon honey
3 tablespoons Grand Marnier
2 tablespoons cornflour mixed with
   1 tablespoon water

Place spinach, butter and nuts in a microwave-safe dish and cook covered on high (100%) for 2 minutes. Spread over meat, roll up and secure with string. Elevate pork in a microwave-safe baking dish. Cook on medium-high (70%) for 56 minutes or 14 minutes per 500 g.

Remove and keep warm.

Cut pork rind into pieces 3 cm × 3 cm, place on 4 layers of paper towel and sprinkle generously with salt. Place 2 layers of paper towel over rind. Cook elevated on high (100%) for 4–5 minutes or until rind puffs up.

To make sauce, combine water, stock cube, vinegar, honey, Grand Marnier and cornflour and water mixture. Cook on high (100%) for 4–5 minutes, stirring halfway through cooking. Serve pork cut in slices, spoon over sauce. Garnish with orange twists and crackling puffs.

Serves 6 M

To make beautiful pork crackling, sprinkle generously with salt and cook between several layers of paper towel on high until it puffs up.

Left to right: Medallions of Pork with Ginger Sauce and Grand Marnier Pork with Crackling Puffs

Glazed Spareribs and Pork Kebabs

PORK KEBABS

15 g butter
500 g pork steak, diced
1 medium-sized fresh pineapple, skinned
170 g jar ginger in syrup, diced,
 reserving 1 piece
1 red capsicum, diced
bamboo skewers, dipped in oil
¼ cup cream
fresh chives

Preheat a 25 cm browning dish on high (100%) for 8 minutes. Add butter and swirl to coat dish. Add pork, turning to sear. Cook on high (100%) for 4–5 minutes, turning halfway through cooking.

Dice about ¼ of the pineapple. Thread diced pork, ginger, capsicum and pineapple onto bamboo skewers until all skewers are full. Place 6 skewers at a time on a microwave-safe roasting rack. Cook on high (100%) for 5–6 minutes or until cooked.

Chop remaining pineapple and place it with the reserved piece of ginger and 2 tablespoons of ginger syrup in a food processor. Process until smooth, stir in cream and cook in a microwave-safe jug on medium-high (70%) for 2–3 minutes or until just heated.

To serve, pour some sauce on a plate with 2 skewers per person. Top with finely chopped chives.

Serves 6 ⬚M

GLAZED SPARERIBS

1 kg pork spareribs

Marinade
¾ cup Hoi Sin Sauce
1 tablespoon oil
1 tablespoon soy sauce
1 tablespoon honey
1 clove garlic, crushed
1 teaspoon finely chopped fresh ginger root

Combine Hoi Sin Sauce, oil, soy sauce, honey, garlic and ginger. Cook on high (100%) for 30 seconds. Toss spareribs in marinade and stand for 2 hours. Drain, reserving marinade.

Arrange spareribs in a shallow microwave-safe dish, cover, and cook on high (100%) for 10 minutes, then on medium (50%) for 10 minutes. Heat marinade on high (100%) for 1 minute. Serve spareribs on a decorative plate and pour over heated marinade.

Serves 8 ⬚M

SESAME PORK TENDERLOIN

1 kg whole pork tenderloin, bone
 removed
⅔ cup water
½ cup soy sauce
2 shallots, finely chopped
1 tablespoon oil
1 clove garlic, crushed
2.5 cm piece fresh ginger root, finely
 chopped
2 tablespoons toasted sesame seeds

Place tenderloin in a 2 litre microwave-safe casserole. Combine water, soy sauce, shallots, oil, garlic and ginger and pour over meat. Sprinkle sesame seeds on pork. Cover and cook on medium-high (70%), allowing 9 minutes per 500 g of pork. Turn pork over halfway through cooking and baste it with sauce.

To serve, cut into thin slices, cutting across the pork i.e. from the rind to where the bone would be had it not been removed. Serve on a bed of rice.

Serves 6 ⬚M

51

Plates Studio-Haus

Veal Escalopes with Fennel

MEXICAN BEEF CASSEROLE

1 kg chuck steak, diced
½ cup flour
1 red capsicum, cut into strips
1 green capsicum, cut into strips
1 onion, sliced
1 chilli, finely chopped
425 g canned tomatoes in juice
2 cups beef stock
250 g canned corn kernels

Toss meat in flour. Place all ingredients except corn in a microwave-safe dish and mix to combine. Cover dish and cook.

To cook by micro/convection
Panasonic: Combination 3 for
          1 hour
Sharp: High-Mix 160°C for
          1 hour
Sanyo: Micro/convection 160°C
          for 45 minutes

Add corn kernels 15 minutes before completion of cooking.

Serves 6   `M/C`

WHOLE BAKED SNAPPER

Stuffing
1 onion, finely chopped
50 g butter, melted
2 tablespoons chopped celery
2 tablespoons chopped fresh parsley
2 cups soft breadcrumbs
2 tablespoons chopped fresh dill

Snapper
2 kg snapper, cleaned and scaled
juice 1 lemon
paprika
chopped fresh dill
sprig fresh parsley, to garnish

Combine all stuffing ingredients and mix well. Remove eyes from fish and insert stuffing in cavity of fish. Squeeze lemon juice and sprinkle over with paprika and dill. Wrap a shield of foil over head and tail and place in a large microwave-safe dish. Cook on high (100%) for 10 minutes. Arrange a sprig of parsley in the eye socket to garnish.

Serves 4   `M`

PEPPERED PORK WITH MUSHROOMS

40 g butter
4–6 large butterfly pork chops or pork
  fillets
1 tablespoon flour
200 g mushroom caps, sliced
2 tablespoons green peppercorns,
  crushed
½ cup shallots, sliced
½ cup cream

Preheat a large browning dish on high (100%) for 6 minutes. Add half the butter and swirl to coat dish. Add chops, turning to sear. Then cook on high (100%) for 6 minutes, turning halfway through cooking time. Remove chops and reserve juices.

Add remaining butter and flour to dish. Stir to combine. Cook on high (100%) for 1 minute. Add mushrooms, peppercorns and shallots, and cook on high (100%) for 3 minutes. Add cream and stir well. Cook on high (100%) for a further 1 minute. Pour sauce over chops and serve.

Serves 4–6   `M`

VEAL ESCALOPES WITH FENNEL

40 g butter
500 g veal escalopes, tossed in flour
12 spring onions (see Note)
fennel leaves, finely chopped
lemon juice
chopped fresh parsley

Preheat a microwave-safe 25 cm casserole browning dish on high (100%) for 8 minutes. Add butter, and swirl to coat dish. Sear veal on both sides then add onions. Cook on high (100%) for 4 minutes, turning after 2 minutes. After stirring, cover and cook on high (100%) for 3 minutes. Add fennel leaves, lemon juice and parsley. Cook on high (100%) for 1 minute and serve.
Note: Use round-bulbed spring onions, not thin shallots.

Serves 4   `M`

VEAL CAMPAGNOLA

1 clove garlic, crushed
25 g butter
400 g canned tomatoes, drained
  (reserve liquid)
2 tablespoons red wine
1 tablespoon brown sugar
freshly ground black pepper
100 g spinach leaves, washed and
  shredded
4 veal steaks
4 slices Edam cheese

Place garlic and 20 g butter in a 2 litre microwave-safe casserole dish and cook on high (100%) for 1 minute. Add drained tomatoes, ¼ cup reserved liquid, wine, sugar and pepper. Cook on high (100%) for 8 minutes and remove. Cook spinach in a freezer bag on high (100%) for 1 minute, remove and combine with tomato mixture.

Preheat a 25 cm browning dish on high (100%) for 6 minutes. Add extra 5 g butter, swirl to coat. Add veal, turning to sear. Cook on high (100%) for 2 minutes. Turn veal over. Divide spinach and tomato mixture into 4 and place on top of each steak. Top each steak with a slice of cheese. Cover and cook on medium (50%) for 10 minutes.

Serves 4 | M |

Veal Campagnola

SPICY PRAWNS

1 kg prawns, shelled and deveined

Marinade
½ cup polyunsaturated oil
½ cup cider vinegar
1 tablespoon tomato sauce
1 clove garlic, crushed
3 tablespoons finely chopped fresh
  parsley
1 shallot, finely chopped
freshly ground black pepper
dash Tabasco
pinch cayenne pepper

Combine marinade ingredients. Add prawns and mix until they're well coated. Chill for 2 hours. Drain prawns and reserve marinade.

Preheat a 25 cm casserole browning dish on high (100%) for 8 minutes. Swirl 1 tablespoon of marinade in the browning dish. Add prawns, stir then cook on high (100%) for 4–5 minutes, stirring once during cooking. Serve on a bed of rice.

Serves 4 | M |

BEEF PEBRONATA

500 g blade steak, diced
2 tablespoons flour
½ cup beef stock
1 cup white wine
fresh parsley, to garnish

Pebronata Sauce
1 onion, sliced
1 capsicum, sliced into strips
2 cloves garlic, crushed
½ teaspoon dried thyme
1 tablespoon chopped fresh parsley
2 tablespoons olive oil
1 tablespoon flour
3 medium-sized tomatoes, peeled and
  chopped
½ cup red wine

Toss meat in flour and place in a 2 litre microwave/convection-safe dish. Add beef stock and wine. Cook covered on high (100%) for 10 minutes, then on medium (50%) for 30 minutes. Alternatively, cook by micro/convection (see below).

To cook by micro/convection
Panasonic: Combination 3 for
      30 minutes
Sharp: High-Mix 160°C for
      30 minutes
Sanyo: Micro/convection 160°C
      for 30 minutes.

To make sauce, in a microwave-safe dish combine and cook onion, capsicum, garlic, thyme, parsley and oil on high (100%) for 6 minutes, stirring once during cooking. Stir in flour then add tomatoes and wine. Cook on high (100%) for 4 minutes, stirring halfway through the cooking.

Stir sauce into meat mixture. Cover and cook on medium (50%) for 5 minutes. Serve garnished with parsley.

Serves 4 | M | or | M/C |

THE WONDERFUL WORLD OF VEGIES

As every microwave cook knows, microwaved vegetables are delicious when prepared and cooked properly. In this section, you can find everything from Dauphinoise Potatoes and Curried Mushrooms to Spicy Bean Salad and Steamed Snow Peas.

Clockwise from top: Spicy Bean Salad, Dauphinoise Potatoes and Layered Vegetable Terrine

FRESH VEGETABLE COOKING CHART

VEGETABLE	AMOUNT	COOKING TIME ON HIGH (100%)
Asparagus	500 g	5–6 minutes
Beans	500 g	8–10 minutes
Broccoli	500 g	4–5 minutes
Brussels sprouts	500 g	5–6 minutes
Cabbage	500 g	4–5 minutes
Capsicum	500 g	5–6 minutes
Carrots	500 g	10–12 minutes
Cauliflower	500 g	6–8 minutes
Celery	2 stalks	2 minutes
Corn	1 cob	2 minutes
Eggplant	500 g	5–6 minutes
Mushrooms	500 g	5 minutes
Onions	500 g	5 minutes
Peas	500 g	5 minutes
Potatoes	500 g	10–12 minutes
Pumpkin	500 g	10–12 minutes
Spinach	250 g	3–5 minutes
Sweet potatoes	500 g	8–10 minutes
Tomatoes	500 g	5 minutes
Zucchini	250 g	3–4 minutes
ALL FROZEN VEGETABLES Regardless of Type	500 g	8 minutes

VEGETABLE TIPS FOR SUCCESS

- Always cook covered.
- Always choose a container that is the correct size for the amount of vegetables being cooked.
- Remember excess air will toughen vegetables.
- Do NOT add salt until cooked as it will also toughen vegetables.
- A little water may be added to fresh vegetables before cooking.
- Too much water will increase the cooking time.
- Weigh your vegetables to determine the correct cooking time.
- If you halve the weight, halve the time.

LAYERED VEGETABLE TERRINE

700 g carrots, peeled and sliced
300 g parsnips, peeled and sliced
2 bunches spinach, washed and white stalks removed
6 eggs
3/4 cup cream
freshly ground black pepper

Cook carrots in freezer bag on high (100%) for 8 minutes. Cook parsnips in freezer bag on high (100%) for 5 minutes. Cook spinach in freezer bag on high (100%) 7 minutes. Allow to cool slightly and squeeze dry.

Puree carrots with 2 eggs, 1/4 cup cream and pepper. Spread mixture evenly over the base of a microwave/convection plastic loaf container (12 cm × 26 cm).

Puree spinach with 2 eggs, 1/4 cup cream and pepper. Spread in a layer over the carrot. Puree parsnips with 2 eggs, 1/4 cup cream and pepper. Spread over spinach. Cook and serve in slices.

Cook elevated on micro/convection

Panasonic:	Combination 3 for 30 minutes
Sharp:	High-Mix 160°C for 30 minutes
Sanyo:	Micro/convection 160°C for 25 minutes

Makes 15 slices M/C

SPICY BEAN SALAD

500 g stringless beans, washed
1 teaspoon water
1 onion, diced
1/2 red capsicum, sliced
1 clove garlic, crushed
1/4 teaspoon chilli powder
10 g butter
1/4 cup sultanas
250 g mushrooms, sliced

Place beans and water in a freezer bag. Cook on high (100%) for 4 minutes. Combine onion, capsicum, garlic, chilli powder and butter in a small microwave-safe casserole dish and cook on high (100%) for 2 minutes. Add in beans, sultanas and mushrooms then stir gently. Cover and cook on high (100%) for 2 minutes.

Serves 6 M

FANNED GLAZED CARROTS

6 baby carrots, peeled
2 tablespoons honey
20 g butter

Cook carrots in a freezer bag on high (100%) for 3–4 minutes. Place honey and butter in bag, toss well to coat carrots. Cut each carrot into thin slices vertically to within 0.5 cm of the base, fan out slightly and serve.

Serves 6 M

Carrot Timbales with Fanned Glazed Carrots

DAUPHINOISE POTATOES

500 g new potatoes, peeled and thinly sliced
1 onion, sliced
1 cup sour cream
250 g bacon, diced
½ cup grated cheese
1 teaspoon chopped fresh parsley
paprika (for microwave only)

Place layers of potato and onion in a shallow micro/convection-safe container. Cover and cook on high (100%) for 8 minutes. Spread with sour cream. Top with sprinkled bacon, cheese and parsley. Cook on high (100%) for 5 minutes. Sprinkle with paprika and serve. Alternatively, cook by micro/convection (see below).

To cook by micro/convection
Preheat oven to 230°C.

Panasonic:	Combination 4 for 15 minutes
Sharp:	Low-Mix 230°C for 10–12 minutes
Sanyo:	Micro/convection 230°C for 13–14 minutes

Serves 6   M   or   M/C

CARROT TIMBALES

500 g carrots, peeled and sliced
dash cinnamon
freshly ground black pepper
4 eggs, lightly beaten
6 tiny cherry tomatoes
chives, to garnish

Cook carrots in a freezer bag on high (100%) for 6 minutes. Allow to cool. Puree carrots with cinnamon and pepper and fold in eggs. Divide mixture between 6 lightly greased individual ramekins (½ cup capacity). Cook on medium-low (30%) for 6 minutes or until set. Turn onto serving plate and top each with a cherry tomato and a sprinkle of chives.

Serves 6   M

Plate Villa Italiana

PARSLEY-DIPPED SAVOURY BACON POTATOES

4 medium-sized potatoes, scrubbed
1 tablespoon mayonnaise
1 tablespoon sour cream
¼ teaspoon French mustard
1 egg yolk
2 bacon rashers, finely chopped
finely chopped fresh parsley
melted butter

Pierce skin of potatoes with a knife several times. Cook on high (100%) for 10–12 minutes. Slice 1 cm off top of potatoes. Scoop out the centres leaving 1 cm of potato around sides. Mash together potato, mayonnaise, sour cream, mustard and egg yolk. Spoon mixture back into potato shells. Sprinkle each potato with bacon. Cook on high (100%) for 2–3 minutes. Alternatively, cook by micro/convection (see below).

To cook by micro/convection
Preheat oven to 230°C.

Panasonic:	Combination 4 for 15 minutes
Sharp:	Low-Mix 230°C for 10 minutes
Sanyo:	Micro/convection 230°C for 10 minutes

Brush potatoes with melted butter and dip in parsley to serve.

Serves 4   M or M/C

Parsley-dipped Savoury Bacon Potatoes

CURRIED MUSHROOMS

60 g butter
2 onions, sliced
3 teaspoons curry powder
250 g button mushrooms
410 g canned whole tomatoes, drained, reserve half the juice
½ cup chicken stock
½ cup sour cream

Combine butter and onions in a 2 litre microwave-safe casserole dish. Cook on high (100%) for 3 minutes. Add curry powder and cook on high (100%) for 1 minute. Add mushrooms and cook on high (100%) for 2 minutes. Add tomatoes, reserved juice and stock. Cook on high (100%) for 2–3 minutes. Stir through sour cream. Serve on a bed of rice.

Serves 6   M

FANNED POTATOES

6 medium-sized potatoes, peeled
50 g butter, melted
paprika

Cut potatoes into thin slices, lengthways, leaving 0.5 cm on the base uncut so slices are still attached. Place potatoes on a microwave-safe baking tray, brush with butter and sprinkle with paprika. Preheat oven to 220°C.

To cook by micro/convection

Panasonic:	Combination 4 for 37 minutes
Sharp:	High-Mix 220°C for 35 minutes
Sanyo:	Micro/convection 220°C for 35 minutes

Serves 6   M/C

STIR-FRIED VEGETABLES

40 g butter
2 large onions, cut into rings
1 large red capsicum, sliced
1 large green capsicum, sliced
1 carrot, cut into thin strips
4 stalks celery, thinly sliced
2 zucchini, thinly sliced
250 g broccoli, cut into flowerets

Preheat a 25 cm casserole browning dish on high (100%) for 6 minutes. Add butter, onions and capsicums and toss. Cook on high (100%) for 3–4 minutes. Add carrot and cook on high (100%) for 1–2 minutes. Add celery, zucchini and broccoli and cook on high (100%) for 3 minutes.

Serves 6   M

Stir-fried Vegetables

COUNTRY GREEN BROCCOLI

500 g broccoli, cut into flowerets
1 teaspoon water

Place broccoli in a freezer bag, add water and shake. Twist the end of the freezer bag and tuck it underneath. Cook on high (100%) for 4–5 minutes.

Serves 6

BEAN BUNDLES TIED WITH DILL

150 g stringless beans, washed
20 g butter
fresh dill

Place beans and butter in a freezer bag. Twist the top and tuck it underneath the bag. Cook on high (100%) for 2 minutes. Divide beans into 4 bundles. Tie each bundle with a piece of dill.

Serves 4

SWEET AND SOUR CAPSICUMS WITH CASHEWS

1 red capsicum, cut into 5 mm strips
1 green capsicum, cut into 5 mm strips
1 onion, sliced
½ cup cashew nuts, roasted

Sauce
¼ cup white vinegar
½ cup sugar
1 tablespoon tomato sauce
1 tablespoon soy sauce
1 tablespoon cornflour combined with
*   ½ cup water*

Combine sauce ingredients in a microwave-safe jug and cook on high (100%) for 3 minutes. Stir after 2 minutes. Place capsicums and onion in a 1 litre microwave-safe casserole dish. Cover and cook on high (100%) for 5 minutes, stirring once. Add sauce and stir to coat vegetables. Just before serving, sprinkle with cashew nuts.

Serves 4

RED CABBAGE AND BACON HOT POT

6 bacon rashers, rind removed
½ small red cabbage, shredded
1 onion, finely chopped
3 tablespoons malt vinegar
3 tablespoons redcurrant jelly
1 tablespoon sesame seeds
nutmeg
freshly ground black pepper

Roll up each bacon rasher. Place in a microwave-safe casserole dish. Combine remaining ingredients and spoon on top of bacon rolls. Cover and cook until tender.

To cook by micro/convection

Panasonic:	Combination 4 for	
	45 minutes	
Sharp:	High-Mix at 180°C for	
	45 minutes	
Sanyo:	Micro/convection 180°C	
	for 30 minutes	

Serves 6

PUMPKIN IN SWISS CHEESE SAUCE

1 pumpkin, approximately 17 cm in
*   diameter*
140 g butter, softened
¼ teaspoon nutmeg
freshly ground black pepper
1 onion, finely chopped
1½ cups soft breadcrumbs
½ teaspoon dried mixed herbs
½ cup Swiss cheese, grated
300 mL sour cream

Cut the top off the pumpkin. Remove the seeds and soft centre. Mix together 40 g butter, nutmeg and pepper. Smear the inside of the pumpkin and its lid with the mixture.

Cook remaining butter and the onion on high (100%) for 1½ minutes. Add combined breadcrumbs, herbs and cheese and spoon into pumpkin. Pour in sour cream. Replace the lid and cook on high (100%) for 30 minutes or until pumpkin is tender. To serve, cut pumpkin in slices and spoon over sauce.

Serves 6

CAULIFLOWER PROVENCAL

500 g cauliflower, cut into flowerets
½ cup grated cheese

Sauce
1 tablespoon oil
1 clove garlic, crushed
1 onion, chopped
425 g canned tomatoes, reserving all
*   juice in can*
freshly ground black pepper
1 tablespoon Worcestershire sauce
pinch dried marjoram

Place cauliflower in a shallow microwave-safe dish. Cover and cook on high (100%) for 6–8 minutes.

To make sauce, in a microwave-safe jug combine oil, garlic and onion. Cook on high (100%) for 3 minutes. Stir in tomatoes and juice, pepper, Worcestershire sauce and marjoram. Cook on high (100%) for 2–3 minutes. Pour sauce over cauliflower, sprinkle with cheese and cook on high (100%) for 1 minute.

Serves 6

CAULIFLOWER AU GRATIN

500 g cauliflower, cut into flowerets
20 g butter
1 tablespoon flour
1 cup milk
¼ cup grated cheese
2 tablespoons chopped fresh parsley

Place cauliflower in a microwave-safe ovenproof dish and cover. Cook on high (100%) for 4 minutes. In a microwave-safe jug melt butter on high (100%) for 30 seconds then stir in flour. Gradually add milk. Cook on high (100%) for 3–4 minutes or until sauce thickens. Stir twice during cooking.

Pour sauce over cauliflower then sprinkle with cheese and parsley. Cook until golden brown.

To cook by micro/convection
Preheat oven to 230°C.

Panasonic:	Combination 4 for	
	15 minutes	
Sharp:	Low-Mix at 230°C for	
	10–12 minutes	
Sanyo:	Micro/convection at	
	230°C for 13–15	
	minutes	

Garnish with parsley and serve.

Serves 4

Cauliflower Provencal and
Red Cabbage and Bacon Hot Pot

MUSHROOM PUFFS

Puffs
1 cup water
40 g butter
1 cup flour
4 eggs

Mushroom Filling
350 g mushrooms, finely sliced
20 g butter
3 tablespoons flour
2 tablespoons sherry
1 cup beef stock
2 tablespoons tomato sauce
freshly ground black pepper

Combine water and butter in a microwave-safe jug. Cook on high (100%) for 3 minutes or until water boils. Using a wooden spoon, beat in flour. Cook on high (100%) for 3 minutes. With an electric beater, beat in eggs one at a time. Beat until mixture is smooth and shiny.

Preheat convection oven to 230°C. Place 6 large spoonfuls of mixture onto a greased pizza tray using heated spoons. Cook elevated on convection at 200°C for 15 minutes. Cook for a further minute on 180°C. Make a 2–3 cm slit, horizontally, in the side of each puff. Return to hot, turned-off oven for 10 minutes.

Place mushrooms and butter in a microwave-safe jug and cook on high (100%) for 3 minutes. Mix in flour, add remaining ingredients and stir. Cook on high (100%) for 3–4 minutes or until mixture thickens, stirring once. Cut a lid off each puff and scrape out damp centre with a fork. Fill each puff with mushroom filling and replace lid.

Note: For those without a micro/convection oven, choux pastry can be cooked in a conventional oven.

Makes 6   M   and   C

MINTED NEW POTATOES

500 g small new potatoes
40 g butter
3 tablespoons chopped fresh mint

Place potatoes in a microwave-safe shallow dish and cover. Cook on high (100%) for 8 minutes. Toss in butter and mint. Cook on high (100%) for 1 minute.

Serves 6   M

Mushroom Puffs

STUFFED EGGPLANT

1 medium-sized eggplant
salt
1 tablespoon olive oil
1 onion, diced
1 clove garlic, crushed
2 tomatoes, peeled and chopped
1 zucchini, sliced
¼ cup white wine
¼ cup tomato juice
freshly ground black pepper
1 tablespoon chopped fresh basil
½ cup grated cheese
fresh parsley, to garnish

Cut eggplant in half lengthways. Spoon out flesh, being careful not to break the skin. Sprinkle shells with salt and place shells face down on a plate while preparing filling.

Chop eggplant flesh. Combine oil, onion and garlic and cook on high (100%) for 2 minutes. Add eggplant flesh and cook on high (100%) for 5 minutes or until eggplant is tender. Add tomatoes, zucchini, wine, tomato juice, pepper and basil then cook on high (100%) for 5 minutes or until most of the liquid is absorbed.

Rinse the shells, pat them dry and brush with olive oil. Place shells upside down in a microwave-safe casserole dish. Cover and cook on high (100%) for 3–4 minutes or until shells are soft. Place filling in shells and sprinkle with grated cheese. Cook on high (100%) for 1–2 minutes, or until cheese has melted. Serve sprinkled with parsley.

Serves 2

To dry your own herbs and spices, place between paper towel, cook on high (100%) until dry, rub between hands and store.

To dry bread for croutons or breadcrumbs place 120 g bread cubed into a glass dish. Cook on high (100%) for 4–5 minutes or until dry, stirring occasionally.

Blanch nuts by heating in boiling water on high (100%) for 1 minute.

HOT POTATO SALAD

500 g potatoes, peeled and diced
1 teaspoon water
2 chicken stock cubes, crushed
1 onion, diced
4 rashers bacon, diced
½ cup sour cream
¼ cup mayonnaise
¼ teaspoon mustard powder
¼ teaspoon paprika

Place potatoes in a shallow microwave-safe dish. Sprinkle with water and crushed stock cubes. Cover and cook on high (100%) for 6 minutes, then drain.

Place onion and bacon in a microwave-safe jug. Cook on high (100%) for 2 minutes then drain. Add sour cream, mayonnaise, mustard and paprika and mix to combine. Fold this through the potatoes. Cook on high (100%) for 3 minutes. Serve hot or cold.

Serves 6

POTATO BAKE

1 tablespoon flour
1 cup milk
1 egg
2 large potatoes, cooked and peeled
1 cup grated tasty cheese
4 rashers bacon, diced
1 red capsicum, cut into thin strips
1 large onion, thinly sliced into rings
1 tablespoon chopped fresh rosemary
2 tablespoons chopped fresh parsley
freshly ground black pepper

Preheat convection oven to 220°C. Mix together flour, milk and egg to form a thin paste.

Layer potatoes, cheese, bacon, capsicum, onion, herbs, pepper and thin paste into 18 cm souffle dish. Repeat until all ingredients are used and dish is filled. Cook and serve.

To cook by micro/convection

Panasonic:	Combination 4 for 25 minutes
Sharp:	High-Mix 220°C for 20 minutes
Sanyo:	Micro/convection 220°C for 15 minutes

Serves 5

ZUCCHINI AND CARROTS JULIENNE

150 g zucchini, cut into matchstick size
    pieces
150 g carrots, cut into matchstick size
    pieces
1 tablespoon orange juice
1 teaspoon chopped fresh parsley

Place zucchini and carrots in a shallow microwave-safe dish. Cover and cook on high (100%) for 5 minutes. Pour over orange juice and sprinkle with parsley. Mix well and serve.

Serves 6

STEAMED SNOW PEAS

150 g snow peas, topped and tailed

Place snow peas in a freezer bag and remove excess air. Cook on high (100%) for 1½ minutes.

Serves 4 [M]

ZUCCHINI CASSEROLE

500 g zucchini, sliced
2 tomatoes, peeled and diced
2 onions, diced
40 g butter
1 clove garlic, crushed

Place all ingredients in a shallow dish, cover and cook on high (100%) for 6 minutes. Toss to combine.

Serves 6 [M]

SWEET TEMPTATIONS

For a party, afternoon tea or morning coffee, everyone enjoys something sweet. With your microwave, you can enjoy hours of fun experimenting with cakes, meringues, pies, tarts, tortes, souffles, slices, chocolate dipped fruit and biscuits, to celebrate any occasion with flair.

Clockwise from top: Mille Feuilles, Matchsticks, Fruit Flambe, and Rum and Chocolate Mocca Gateau

Cake plate David Jones   Plate and glass Holmegaard   Cake stand Dansab

Boysenberry Delight and Fruit Tartlets

FRUIT TARTLETS

Pastry
60 g butter
150 g flour
1 tablespoon caster sugar
1 egg yolk
water

Filling
¾ cup sugar
5 egg yolks
⅓ cup flour, sifted
1 ¾ cups milk
20 g butter
¼ teaspoon vanilla essence
¼ teaspoon almond essence

Topping
2 × 250 g punnets strawberries
12 apricot halves
3 kiwi fruit, sliced
½ cup apricot juice
1 tablespoon gelatine
1 teaspoon apricot jam

Place butter and flour into food processor and process until mixture resembles fine breadcrumbs. Continue to process while adding sugar, egg yolk and sufficient water to bind pastry and give a soft

dough. Turn pastry out onto a lightly floured surface and knead lightly. Wrap in plastic wrap and chill for 30 minutes.

Roll pastry out thinly. Using a pastry cutter, cut 12 rounds about 6 cm in diameter. Place six rounds into a microwave-safe muffin tray. Prick base of each shell twice with a fork. Cook elevated on high (100%) for 3 minutes. Repeat with remaining six rounds. Allow to cool before filling. Alternatively, cook by micro/convection (see below).

To cook by micro/convection
Preheat oven to 200°C.
Prepare pastry as above. Cut into rounds and press into six-hole metal patty pan trays. Place one tray on a wire rack and the other underneath.

Panasonic:	Combination 4 for 10 minutes, exchange trays, cook on combination 4 for a further 5 minutes or until golden
Sharp:	High-Mix 200°C for 10 minutes, exchange trays, cook on High-Mix for a further 5 minutes or until golden
Sanyo:	Micro/Convection 200°C for 8 minutes, exchange trays, cook for a further 5 minutes on Micro/Convection 200°C or until golden

To make filling, beat sugar into egg yolks until light and fluffy. Beat in sifted flour. Place milk in a large microwave-safe jug. Cook on high (100%) for 3–4 minutes or until milk begins to boil. Gradually beat milk into egg yolk mixture. Cook on high (100%) for 2 minutes or until mixture begins to boil. Add butter and essences, continue to beat until mixture is shiny. Chill slightly. Spread filling into each pastry shell. Cool.

Top each tartlet with a selection of strawberries, apricot halves and kiwi fruit. Combine apricot juice and gelatine in a cup, cook on high (100%) for 45 seconds or until gelatine dissolves. Add jam, stir to combine. Brush generously over fruit.

Makes 12   [M] or [M/C]

BOYSENBERRY DELIGHT

850 g canned boysenberries, reserve all juice
2 tablespoons gelatine
2 cups thickened cream
½ cup icing sugar

Drain boysenberries, reserving both juice and fruit. Add gelatine to juice and cook in a microwave-safe jug on high (100%) for 1 minute. Cool slightly. Place reserved boysenberries in blender and process until smooth. Add juice/gelatine mixture and blend until combined.

Beat cream and icing sugar together until stiff. Fold through boysenberry mixture. Pour into a 20 cm ring mould and chill for 1 hour.

Serves 8–10 `M`

MATCHSTICKS

25 cm × 25 cm piece prepared puff pastry
½ cup raspberry jam
1 cup cream, whipped

Icing
2 cups icing sugar
10 g butter
1 ½ tablespoons water

Decoration
100 g dark chocolate
1 teaspoon copha

Preheat oven to 230°C. Halve pastry sheet and cook following the recipe for Mille Feuilles. Spread raspberry jam over the flat side of one piece of pastry and top with whipped cream.

To make icing, combine icing sugar with butter. Heat water on high (100%) for 40 seconds, and pour into the icing sugar. Mix until smooth. Spread icing sugar over the flat side of the remaining pastry sheet.

Place chocolate and copha in a microwave-safe jug. Cook on high 1–2 minutes or until chocolate has melted. Stir until smooth. Using a small nozzle, pipe chocolate in thin lines about 2.5 cm apart, across icing. While chocolate is still soft run the back of a knife gently down icing, lengthways. Keeping lines about 2 cm apart, draw knife up the icing in the opposite direction. Repeat this step until icing is covered with a decorative feather pattern.

Allow to set. Place iced pastry sheet on cream.

Leave icing and chocolate to set. Using a sharp knife, cut into 6 strips and serve.

Makes 6 `M/C`

MILLE FEUILLES

25 cm × 25 cm piece prepared puff pastry
1 cup cream, whipped
1 tablespoon Kirsch
125 g raspberries, hulled
½ cup icing sugar

Preheat oven to 230°C. Cut pastry sheet in half and place each half on microwave-safe scone tray lined with baking paper. Using a fork, prick pastry all over. Refrigerate for at least 10 minutes or until ready to use.

Place one scone tray on a wire elevation rack in the oven. Place the other scone tray underneath. Cook until top sheet is puffed and lightly browned.

To cook by micro/convection

Panasonic:	Combination 4 for 6 minutes	
Sharp:	High-Mix 230°C for 5 minutes	
Sanyo:	Micro/convection 240°C for 4 minutes	

Remove top pastry sheet and cool on a wire rack. Place lower pastry sheet onto elevation rack. Cook until remaining pastry sheet is puffed and slightly browned.

To cook by micro/convection

Panasonic:	Combination 4 for 3 minutes	
Sharp:	High-Mix 230°C for 2 minutes	
Sanyo:	Micro/convection 240°C for 2 minutes	

Place second pastry sheet on a wire rack to cool. When cold cut each sheet, widthways, into six equal strips. Combine cream and Kirsch. Spread half the cream mixture over six pastry strips, top with raspberries and remaining cream. Place six remaining pastry strips on top. Sift icing sugar over the top and serve.

Makes 6 `M/C`

RUM AND CHOCOLATE MOCCA GATEAU

200 g butter
1 cup sugar
4 tablespoons cocoa
3 cups self-raising flour
2 cups milk
2 teaspoons vanilla essence
4 eggs
1 teaspoon instant coffee
1 tablespoon rum
½ cup boiling water

Chocolate Cream
1 ¼ cups cream, whipped
2 tablespoons cocoa

Topping
20 g copha
375 g dark cooking chocolate
icing sugar, to sprinkle

Preheat oven to 180°C. Grease and line 2 × 20 cm microwave-safe sandwich cake tins. Place butter, sugar and cocoa in a microwave-safe jug. Cook on high (100%) for 45 seconds or until butter melts. Stir to blend. Add flour, milk, vanilla and eggs. Beat for 2 minutes.

Divide mixture into quarters. Pour one-quarter into each sandwich tin. Place a wire elevation rack into the oven, with one sandwich tin on the rack and the other underneath.

To cook by micro/convection
Swap position of cake tins halfway through cooking.

Panasonic:	Combination 4 for 11 minutes	
Sharp:	Low-Mix 180°C for 8 minutes	
Sanyo:	Micro/Convection 180°C for 8 minutes	

Turn cakes out onto wire racks to cool. Repeat with remaining cake mixture. Combine coffee, rum and water. Sprinkle over each layer of cooked cake.

Combine cream and cocoa, spread this chocolate cream on three layers of cake and sandwich layers together. Use the last of the chocolate cream to spread on top of cake and allow to set.

Place copha and cooking chocolate in a microwave-safe jug and cook on high (100%) for 1½–2 minutes or until melted. Stir until smooth.

Cut a piece of baking paper the size of the circumference of the cake. Fold it over widthways until it is the same height as the cake. Spread half the chocolate copha mix over paper and when it is almost set, wrap around cake. Gently remove paper and mould chocolate with hands to fit cake.

Pour remaining chocolate onto a marble slab or chopping board. Make chocolate scrolls by sliding knife firmly along chocolate at 45° angle. Place scrolls on top of the cake.

Serves 10 `M/C`

Remember the cooking time depends on the amount of food being cooked; if you're cooking double the quantity, then double the time.

FRUIT FLAMBE

60 g butter
⅓ cup sugar
2 tablespoons lemon juice
¼ cup orange juice
selection of favourite fruit, roughly
    chopped (e.g. strawberries, kiwi fruit,
    melon, tamarillos, grapes)
1 tablespoon brandy
2 tablespoons Grand Marnier

Place butter and sugar in a large microwave-safe bowl. Cook on high (100%) for 45 seconds or until sugar has melted. Add juices and cook on high (100%) for 1–2 minutes or until mixture boils.

Add fruit, and gently toss it in the juices. Cook on high (100%) for 1 minute. Divide fruit into four individual sweet dishes.

Combine brandy and Grand Marnier in a microwave-safe jug. Cook on high (100%) for 30 seconds. Ignite and pour over fruit.

Serves 4

NUT AND CHOCOLATE PEARS

1 cup red wine
1 cup sugar
2 cm cinnamon stick
4 pears, peeled, with stalks left on
375 g dark chocolate
1 tablespoon copha
1 cup crushed nuts
fresh mint leaves, to garnish

Combine wine, sugar and cinnamon in a large microwave-safe casserole dish and cook on high (100%) for 2 minutes or until sugar is dissolved.

Place pears upright in wine mixture and baste. Cover with plastic wrap and cook on high (100%) for 8 minutes or until pears are cooked but firm. Drain well.

Place chocolate and copha in a microwave-safe jug. Cook on high (100%) for 2 minutes or until chocolate has melted. Dip one side of each pear in melted chocolate then crushed nuts. Stand on baking paper to set. Garnish with mint leaves.

Serves 4

CHOCOLATE CHERRY GATEAU

100 g butter
¼ cup sugar
2 tablespoons honey
3 eggs
1 cup self-raising flour
1 tablespoon cocoa
¼ cup walnuts, chopped
½ cup sherry or brandy
100 g glace cherries, chopped
½ cup chocolate chips
1 ¼ cups whipped cream
chocolate leaves, to garnish

Place butter, sugar and honey in a microwave-safe bowl. Cook on high (100%) for 1 minute. Mix in eggs, fold in flour, cocoa and walnuts. Pour into a pudding shaped microwave-safe container and cook on high (100%) for 4–5 minutes. Stand for 5 minutes before turning out.

Allow cake to cool completely, then split cake horizontally into 3 layers. Sprinkle each layer with sherry.

Mix cherries and chocolate chips, reserving a few to decorate, with one-third of the whipped cream. Sandwich cake together with cherry-chocolate cream.

Cover top and outside of cake with remaining cream and decorate with chopped cherries and chocolate chips. Pipe remaining cream around base of cake and garnish with chocolate leaves.

Note: To make chocolate leaves, brush melted chocolate on the back of Camellia leaves. When set, gently peel leaf away.

Serves 8–10

SWISS WALNUT TART

Pastry
3 ½ cups wholemeal flour
½ cup sugar
1 ½ teaspoons grated lemon rind
180 g butter, softened
2 egg yolks
1 tablespoon brandy
water

Filling
1 cup sugar
¼ cup water
2 cups chopped walnuts
60 g butter
⅔ cup thickened cream
2 tablespoons honey
1 tablespoon brandy

Topping
1 egg yolk
1 tablespoon thickened cream
icing sugar, to sprinkle

Preheat oven to 230°C. Combine flour, sugar, lemon rind and butter in food processor and process until mixture resembles fine breadcrumbs. Add egg yolks and brandy to form a dough (if necessary add a little water). Turn out onto a floured surface and knead lightly.

Roll two-thirds of the dough into a 26 cm circle. Press into a greased 20 cm metal flan dish. Prick pastry several times with fork. To keep the sides of the pastry shell from collapsing and the bottom from puffing up, line with baking paper and weight down with uncooked rice. Cook on high (100%) for 2 minutes then on convection at 220°C for 10 minutes. Remove baking paper and rice and cook on convection at 220°C for 5 minutes.

To make filling, combine sugar and water in a microwave-safe jug. Cook on high (100%) for 2–3 minutes to dissolve sugar then stir. Cook on high (100%) for 6–8 minutes or until mixture is a light caramel colour. Stir in walnuts, butter and cream. Mix well and cook on medium (50%) for 5 minutes. Stir in honey and brandy. Spoon filling into pastry base.

Roll remaining dough into strips (20 cm by 1 cm) and arrange over filling in a lattice pattern. Combine egg yolk and cream and brush over lattice. Preheat oven to 220°C.

To cook by micro/convection
Panasonic: Combination 4 for
              15 minutes
Sharp: Low-Mix at 180°C for 15
              minutes
Sanyo: Micro/convection at
              180°C for 10–15
              minutes or until golden
              brown

Serve decorated with sprinkled icing sugar.

Serves 10–12 [M/C]

HOW TO MIX A MICROWAVE CAKE

Place dry ingredients in a suitable sized bowl. Make a well in the centre of the dry ingredients, place wet ingredients into the well and mix to combine. If creaming is necessary, simply soften butter on high (100%) for 30–40 seconds then cream in sugar and eggs.

*Clockwise from top: Chocolate Cherry
Gateau, Swiss Walnut Tart, and
Nut and Chocolate Pears*

STRAWBERRY FLAN

Pastry Case
1 ½ cups flour
100 g butter
1 tablespoon caster sugar
1 egg yolk
1–2 tablespoons chilled water
1 cup uncooked rice

Creme Patissiere
¾ cup sugar
5 egg yolks
⅓ cup flour, sifted
1 ¾ cups milk
20 g butter
¼ teaspoon vanilla essence

Topping
2 × 250 g punnets strawberries, hulled
1 cup apricot juice
1 tablespoon gelatine
1 tablespoon apricot jam

To make pastry case, place flour and butter in food processor and process until mixture resembles fine breadcrumbs. Continue to process while adding sugar, egg and sufficient water to bind pastry and give a soft dough. Turn pastry out onto a lightly floured surface, knead lightly, wrap in plastic wrap. Chill 30 minutes .

Roll pastry out thinly to fit a 20 cm pie plate. Place into dish, prick base with a fork several times. Place a sheet of baking paper on top of pastry and add uncooked rice. Place a strip of foil around inside upper edge of pastry. Cook elevated on high (100%) for 4–5 minutes. Remove foil, baking paper and rice. Cook for a further 1½–2 minutes on high (100%). Alternatively, cook without foil by micro/convection (see below).

To cook by micro/convection
Preheat oven to 200°C and cook elevated. .

Panasonic:	Combination 4 for 10 minutes, remove baking paper and rice. Cook on Combination 4 for a further 3–5 minutes or until golden.
Sharp:	High-Mix 200°C for 10 minutes, remove baking paper and rice. Cook on High-Mix 200°C for a further 3–5 minutes or until golden.
Sanyo:	Micro/convection 200°C for 10 minutes, remove baking paper and rice. Cook on micro/ convection 200°C for a further 2–3 minutes.

To make Creme Patissiere, beat sugar into egg yolks until light and fluffy then beat in sifted flour. Place milk in a large microwave-safe jug and cook on high (100%) for 3–4 minutes or until milk begins to boil. Gradually beat milk into egg yolk mixture. Cook on high (100%) for 2 minutes or until mixture begins to boil. Add butter and vanilla essence. Beat until shiny. Cool slightly then spread into pastry case and chill.

To make topping, arrange strawberries on top. Combine apricot juice and gelatine in a microwave-safe jug. Cook on high (100%) for 45 seconds–1 minute or until gelatine melts. Add jam, stir to combine and brush apricot glaze over strawberries.

Serves 8–10   M or M/C

SCRUMPTIOUS DESSERT TIPS FOR SUCCESS

- Do NOT use the mixer to mix batters. Combine the ingredients using a whisk or fork. There is no need to mix the mixture until smooth. Incorporating too much air into the batter will cause it to prematurely stale when cooked in the microwave.
- There is no need to sift ingredients.
- Creaming is easy. Simply soften butter in the microwave for 30–40 seconds on high (100%) and add sugar.
- A microwave-safe plastic container gives better results than glass, ceramic or pottery containers. Do NOT grease microwave-safe plastic containers.
- A ring mould container is generally the best to use as this overcomes the problem of having an uncooked centre.

Soften hard ice cream in the microwave for a few seconds.

To soften candied honey, remove lid and cook on high (100%) for 45 seconds.

Rejuvenate stale biscuits or potato crisps by putting them on paper towel and cooking on high (100%) for 45–60 seconds.

Store leftover icing in refrigerator then heat for a few seconds on high (100%) prior to using.

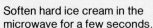

Table mat Jaan Cake plate David Jones

Strawberry Flan

Mousse-filled Chocolate Bags with Exotic Fruit

MOUSSE-FILLED CHOCOLATE BAGS WITH EXOTIC FRUIT

375 g dark chocolate
15 g copha
1 tablespoon Grand Marnier
2 eggs, separated
1 tablespoon sugar
1 ½ cups cream, whipped
exotic fruit (e.g. strawberries,
   blueberries, kiwi fruit)

Cut six sheets of foil to measure 17 cm × 19 cm. Make six foil bags by folding each piece of foil in half, then in half again. Fold raw edge over 0.25 cm, then fold over 0.25 cm again pressing down with fingernail to make a seam. Trim top of bag. Open bag by lifting up one layer of foil, place two fingers inside to gently separate layers of foil.

Place chocolate and copha in a micro-wave-safe jug. Cook on high (100%) for 2 minutes or until chocolate has melted. Stir until smooth. Pour 2 teaspoons of melted chocolate into a foil bag. Using a small paint brush, spread a thin layer of chocolate over bag. Refrigerate until set.

Repeat until foil is evenly coated with chocolate. Repeat with remaining bags.

Add Grand Marnier and egg yolks to remaining chocolate, beating until smooth. Fold whipped cream into chocolate mixture until even in colour. Beat egg whites with sugar until soft peaks form, gently fold into chocolate cream.

Gently remove foil from each chocolate bag. Spoon mousse into each bag. Serve with exotic fruits.

Makes 6

1 Fold each piece of foil in half, then in half again.

2 Fold over raw edge twice.

3 Open bag by gently inserting fingers to lift one layer of foil.

Clockwise from top: Coffee Buttercream Layer Cake, Apricot and Kirsch Souffle and Strawberry Mousse on Sponge

COFFEE BUTTERCREAM LAYER CAKE

1 cup flaked almonds
½ cup caster sugar
4 eggs
½ teaspoon almond essence
2 tablespoons flour
6 egg whites
1 teaspoon instant coffee
⅓ cup boiling water

Coffee Buttercream
4 tablespoons sugar
½ cup hot water
6 egg yolks
300 g butter
1 tablespoon instant coffee

Chocolate Mousse
185 g dark cooking chocolate
⅓ cup milk, boiled
300 mL cream, whipped

Topping
185 g dark cooking chocolate
1 teaspoon butter

Preheat oven to 200°C. Grease and line the bases of two 20 cm square cake tins. Combine almonds, caster sugar, eggs and almond essence. Beat until light and fluffy. Stir in flour. Beat egg whites until stiff then fold into almond mixture.

Divide mixture between the tins. Place a wire elevation rack into oven, placing one cake tin on the rack and the other underneath. Swap position of tins halfway through cooking.

To cook by micro/convection

Panasonic:	Combination 4 for 12 minutes
Sharp:	Low-Mix 200°C for 10 minutes
Sanyo:	Micro/convection 200°C for 9 minutes

Turn cakes out onto greaseproof paper. Dissolve coffee in water and brush over each cake. Cut each cake in half vertically to make four layers.

To make buttercream, cook sugar and water on high (100%) for 8 minutes until it starts to change colour. Pour the hot syrup into egg yolks, beating until thick.

Stand until cool. Beat butter and coffee until light and fluffy then beat into cooled egg yolks.

To make chocolate mousse, break the chocolate into a microwave-safe jug and cook on high (100%) for 1½ minutes or until melted. Stir until smooth. Add hot milk and stir. Cool, then fold in cream.

To assemble, spread half the coffee buttercream evenly over a cake layer. Place another cake layer on top and spread evenly with half the chocolate mousse. Top with another cake layer and spread remaining coffee buttercream evenly over the cake. Top with the last cake layer spread evenly with remaining chocolate mousse. Chill for 2 hours.

To make topping, melt chocolate on high (100%) for 1–1½ minutes or until chocolate has melted. Add butter, stirring until smooth. Spread evenly over the top and sides of cake.

Serves 10   M/C

STRAWBERRY MOUSSE ON SPONGE

1 sponge cake (packet or homemade)
½ cup strawberry jam
1 × 250 g punnet strawberries
1 tablespoon gelatine
⅓ cup water
300 mL cream
½ cup icing sugar
¼ cup icing sugar, extra
200 g chocolate, melted

Prepare and cook sponge. When cold cut sponge horizontally into layers 0.5 cm thick. Using round-based mould or cup, cut six round shapes from sponge. Spread top of each round with strawberry jam.

Reserve six strawberries, puree remaining strawberries. Combine gelatine and water in a microwave-safe jug, and cook on high (100%) for 45 seconds. Stir until combined and add to strawberry puree. Beat together cream and icing sugar until soft peaks form. Reserve ½ cup and fold strawberry puree through remaining cream until well combined. Pour strawberry mixture into six round-based moulds or cups sprinkled with extra icing sugar, filling each cup one-third full. Refrigerate until set.

To serve, place a round of sponge on each plate. Unmould mousse by dipping each mould into warm water, being careful not to wet contents. Invert each mould onto a sponge round. Drizzle melted chocolate on top of each mousse. When chocolate has set, top with whipped cream and a strawberry.

Makes 6 M

APRICOT AND KIRSCH SOUFFLE

315 g packet plain cake mix
1 tablespoon gelatine
½ cup hot water
825 g canned apricot halves, drained and pureed, juice reserved
3 tablespoons orange juice
1 ½ tablespoons lemon juice
2 ½ tablespoons Kirsch
200 mL cream, whipped
2 egg whites
2 tablespoons sugar

Prepare cake according to directions on the packet, substituting reserved apricot juice for milk or water. Place 2 teaspoonsful of cake mix in the bottom of six individual microwave-safe ramekins. Place ramekins in a circle in the oven and cook on high (100%) for 35–40 seconds. Tie a collar of greaseproof paper around each ramekin to extend 3 cm above dish.

Sprinkle gelatine over water, allow to stand for 5 minutes, then cook on high (100%) for 20 seconds. Mix together apricot puree, gelatine mixture, orange and lemon juice and Kirsch. Chill for 45 minutes or until slightly thickened.

Fold in whipped cream. Beat egg whites until soft peaks form. Add sugar and beat until stiff. Fold egg whites into cream mixture. Spoon into ramekins so that mixture comes about 2 cm above the edge of the dish. To level top, tap ramekins gently on the bench. Chill for 3 hours or until set. Decorate with cream and strawberries cut in fan shapes.

Serves 6 M

OPERA HOUSE SPONGE

3 eggs, separated
pinch salt
½ cup caster sugar
¼ teaspoon vanilla essence
⅔ cup cornflour
1 tablespoon flour
1 teaspoon baking powder

Garnish
whipped cream
raspberries

Beat egg whites with salt until soft peaks form. Gradually beat in sugar, a little at a time, then continue to beat until stiff. Add egg yolks and vanilla essence and beat until combined. Sift together cornflour, plain flour and baking powder, three times, then add to egg mixture. Carefully and lightly fold mixture together. Do not stir.

Pour batter into a 18 cm high-sided 2 litre microwave-safe plastic container. Cook elevated on high (100%) for 2½–3 minutes. (See Note.)

Cut a 1 cm slice off top of cooled sponge and cut this slice into four. Decorate cake with whipped cream and raspberries. Stand four sponge pieces at an angle to form Opera House sails, supporting these if necessary with raspberries.

Note: 700 watt microwave ovens will only need 2½ minutes. 600–650 watt microwave ovens will need 3 minutes.

Serves 6 M

Left to right: Apple Rhubarb Tea Cake and Opera House Sponge

APPLE RHUBARB TEA CAKE

4 eggs
1 cup sugar
2/3 cup milk
2 tablespoons brandy
120 g butter, melted
3 cups self-raising flour
2 green apples, peeled, cored and grated
1 green apple, peeled, cored, quartered and sliced

Filling
2 cups stewed rhubarb
1 cup cream, whipped

Grease and line a 20 cm round microwave-safe cake tin. Preheat oven to 180°C. Beat eggs and sugar until creamy. Add milk, brandy, butter, flour and grated apple and mix well. Pour batter into prepared tin. Place apple slices in a decorative pattern on top of batter.

To cook by micro/convection

Panasonic:	Convection 160°C for 5 minutes then Combination 3 for 7 minutes then Convection 160°C for 48 minutes
Sharp:	Convection 160°C for 5 minutes then High-Mix 160°C for 7 minutes then convection 160°C for 50 minutes
Sanyo:	Convection 160°C for 5 minutes then Micro/convection 160°C for 7 minutes then convection 160°C for 35 minutes

Remove from oven and stand for 10 minutes then turn out onto a cooling rack. Combine filling ingredients. Cut cake in half horizontally and sandwich together with filling. Serve in wedges.

Serves 10–12 · M/C

CHERRY ALMOND BRAID

1 1/2 cups milk
60 g butter
1/2 cup sugar
1 tablespoon dried yeast
2 1/4 cups flour
1 teaspoon salt
1 egg yolk, lightly beaten with
1/4 cup milk

Cherry Mixture
60 g butter
1/4 cup flour
200 g glace cherries, finely chopped
100 g slivered almonds

Icing
1 cup icing sugar
water to mix
few drops food colouring

Place milk and 60 g butter in a microwave-safe jug. Cook on medium (50%) for 2–3 minutes or until butter melts. Dissolve 1/2 teaspoon sugar in 1/4 cup warm milk mixture, sprinkle yeast over the top. Cook on defrost (30%) for 10 seconds then stand until yeast froths.

Combine flour, remaining sugar and salt. Mix in yeast mixture and remaining milk. Knead for 7–10 minutes. Place dough in a greased microwave-safe dish, cover with plastic wrap and stand until dough doubles (see *Note*).

To make cherry mixture, combine butter, flour, cherries and almonds. Roll dough, on a lightly floured surface, into a rectangle measuring approximately 30 cm × 23 cm. Place cherry mixture on dough, keeping edges clear. Roll up tightly like a Swiss roll. Roll until dough measures approximately 90 cm. Cut in half lengthways. Braid strips together, keeping cut side up so cherry filling is visible. Form into a circle by gently pressing ends together.

Preheat oven to 220°C. Place braid onto a greased microwave-safe tray. Cover with plastic wrap and allow to rise until double in size. Combine egg and milk then brush over braid.

To cook by micro/convection

Panasonic:	Combination 4 for 8 minutes then convection at 180°C for 10 minutes
Sharp:	Low-Mix at 180°C for 8 minutes then convection at 180°C for 10 minutes
Sanyo:	Micro/convection at 200°C for 6 minutes then convection at 180°C for 10 minutes

Allow to cool. Combine icing sugar with enough water and food colouring to give a very pale pink, watery icing. Drizzle this over braid and decorate with a tiny bunch of flowers and a bow.
Note: To proof dough in the microwave, cook on high (100%) for 15 seconds, then stand for 5 minutes. Repeat until dough has doubled.

Serves 10–12 · M/C

STOLLEN

3/4 cup milk
60 g butter
1/2 cup sugar
1 tablespoon dried yeast
2 1/4 cups flour
1 teaspoon salt
1/2 cup cherries, quartered
1 1/2 cups mixed fruit
1/2 cup slivered almonds
1/2 cup brandy or rum
30 g butter, melted
icing sugar, to sprinkle

Place milk and butter in a microwave-safe dish. Cook on medium (50%) for 2–3 minutes or until butter melts. Dissolve 1/2 teaspoon sugar in 1/2 cup of the warm milk mixture and sprinkle yeast over. Cook this mixture on defrost (30%) for 10 seconds. Let it stand until mixture froths.

Combine flour, remaining sugar, salt, fruit and almonds. Mix in yeast mixture, remaining milk and brandy. Knead for 7–10 minutes. Place dough in a greased microwave-safe bowl, cover it with plastic wrap and proof it until doubled in size.

Using a lightly floured surface, gently roll dough into an oval 25 cm × 30 cm. Fold lengthways, bending slightly to form a moon shape. Preheat oven to 220°C. Place stollen on a greased microwave-safe tray. Cover with plastic wrap, leave to rise until doubled in size. Brush with melted butter.

To cook by micro/convection

Panasonic:	Combination 4 for 8 minutes then convection at 180°C for 10 minutes
Sharp:	Low-Mix at 180°C for 8 minutes then convection at 180°C for 10 minutes
Sanyo:	Micro/convection at 180°C for 6 minutes then convection at 180°C for 10 minutes

Allow to cool completely, then sift icing sugar heavily over stollen and decorate with ribbon.

Serves 8–10 · M/C

Cherry Almond Braid (above) and Stollen (below)

Plate David Jones

Creme Brulee

CHOCOLATE DIPPED HEARTS

250 g butter
½ cup icing sugar
3 cups flour
100 g dark chocolate, melted

Place butter and sugar in food processor and process until creamed. Add flour and continue to process until a soft dough is formed. Roll out to 0.5 cm thickness. Cut into heart-shaped biscuits.

Arrange eight hearts in a circle on greaseproof paper. Cook on high (100%) for 4½ minutes. Remove from microwave and stand on the paper until they cool and become firm and crisp. Repeat with remaining mixture.

When completely cold, dip hearts in chocolate to coat one half of each heart. Place chocolate coated hearts on greaseproof paper to set.

Makes 16

SHORTBREAD HEARTS WITH KIRSCH CREAM AND STRAWBERRY COULIS

2 cups cream, whipped
1 tablespoon Kirsch
1 × 250 g punnet strawberries
12 shortbread hearts (see recipe Chocolate Dipped Hearts)

Combine cream and Kirsch. To make strawberry coulis, puree most of the strawberries until smooth (reserve 2 for garnish). Pour a little strawberry coulis onto each plate. Sandwich together three shortbread hearts, using Kirsch cream as filling. Repeat with remaining hearts. Top with icing sugar, garnish with a swirl of cream and a strawberry half.

Serves 4

> Get more juice from fruits by warming them on high (100%) for 30 seconds. Let them stand for a few minutes before squeezing.

CREME BRULEE WITH SPUN TOFFEE AND TOFFEE DIPPED FRUIT

Creme Brulee
2 cups cream
1 teaspoon vanilla essence
5 egg yolks
4 tablespoons caster sugar
1 tablespoon brandy or rum

Spun Toffee
3 tablespoons sugar
¼ cup hot water

Toffee Dipped Fruit
3 tablespoons sugar
¼ cup hot water
6 strawberries, washed
12 black grapes

To make creme brulee, place cream and vanilla essence in a microwave-safe jug. Cook on medium-high (70%) for 4½ minutes, stirring twice during cooking. Using an electric mixer, beat together egg yolks and caster sugar until fluffy. Add warmed cream very slowly to egg mixture then pour back into jug. Mix in brandy and cook on medium-high (70%) for 3 minutes. Stir and cook on medium (50%) for a further 3½ minutes, stirring after 2 minutes (the mixture should coat a wooden spoon). Pour into 6 individual ramekins. Chill thoroughly.

To make spun toffee, place sugar and water in a microwave-safe jug. Cook on high (100%) for 5–6 minutes until mixture thickens into a golden syrup. Dip a wooden spoon into toffee. Using another wooden spoon, touch spoons and then draw them apart. As toffee strands form, place them on creme brulee.

To make toffee dipped fruit, place sugar and hot water in a microwave-safe jug. Cook on high (100%) for 5–6 minutes until mixture thickens into a golden syrup. Dip fruit into toffee and place on baking paper to set. Serve with creme brulee.

Serves 6

CHOCOLATE AND VANILLA BABY CHOUX

Choux Pastry
1 cup water
40 g butter
1 cup flour
4 eggs
1 egg, lightly beaten

Creme Patissiere
5 egg yolks
¾ cup sugar
⅓ cup flour, sifted
1 ¾ cups milk
20 g butter
1 teaspoon vanilla essence
100 g dark chocolate
1 tablespoon rum

Caramel
2 tablespoons sugar
¼ cup boiling water

Place water and butter in a microwave-safe jug. Cook on high (100%) for 3 minutes or until water boils. Using a wooden spoon, beat in flour. Cook on high (100%) for 3 minutes. Using an electric beater, beat in eggs one at a time. Beat until mixture is smooth and shiny. Preheat convection oven to 220°C.

Using a piping bag with a large nozzle, pipe 12 puffs 2.5 cm in diameter, around a greased microwave-safe pizza tray. Pipe another 12 puffs, 1 cm in diameter, around another greased tray. Gently flatten the top of each puff with the back of a spoon dipped into lightly beaten egg. Place a wire elevation rack in the oven and elevate the larger puffs. Arrange small puffs underneath.

Cook on convection at 200°C for 10 minutes. Remove smaller puffs. Cook larger puffs at 200°C for a further 5 minutes. Make a small slit in the side of each puff. Return both trays to hot, turned-off oven to cool for 5 minutes. Remove from oven and cool completely.

To make Creme Patissiere, beat egg yolks and sugar until light and fluffy. Beat in sifted flour. Place milk in a large microwave-safe jug and cook on high (100%) for 3–4 minutes or until milk begins to boil. Slowly beat milk into egg yolks until mixture is thick and shiny. Cook on high (100%) for 2 minutes or until mixture begins to boil. Beat in butter. Divide mixture into halves and add vanilla to one half. Melt chocolate on high (100%) for 1–1 ½ minutes or until melted then briskly stir in rum. Beat into the other half of the Creme Patissiere.

To fill puffs, place chocolate Creme Patissiere in a piping bag fitted with a small nozzle. Pipe cream into half the large and small puffs through slit. Fill remaining puffs with vanilla Creme Patissiere.

To make caramel, combine sugar and boiling water in a microwave-safe jug, and mix until sugar has dissolved. Cook on high (100%) for 4 minutes or until mixture begins to turn caramel in colour. Cool slightly. Assemble puffs by placing a few drops of caramel over large puffs then sit small puffs on top. Assemble each chou so one puff is chocolate-filled and the other is vanilla-filled.

Note: For those without a micro/convection oven, choux can be cooked in a conventional oven.

Serves 6   M and C

Chocolate Dipped Hearts and Shortbread Hearts with Kirsch Cream and Strawberry Coulis

MANGO MERINGUE GATEAU

Pastry
125 g flour
pinch salt
50 g butter, softened
50 g caster sugar
2 egg yolks, lightly beaten

Meringue
1 egg white
250 g icing sugar

Filling
pulp of 2 mangoes
¼ cup passionfruit pulp
1¼ cups cream, whipped

Place flour, salt, butter and sugar in food processor and process until mixture resembles fine breadcrumbs. Add egg yolks and blend until mixture forms a dough. Turn dough out onto a lightly floured surface. Knead lightly until dough is soft but not sticky. Wrap in plastic wrap and chill for 1 hour. Roll pastry out until .75 cm thick. Cut a 20 cm circle and place on a sheet of greaseproof paper. Cook on high (100%) for 5 minutes. Alternatively, cook by micro/convection (see below).

To cook by micro/convection
Preheat oven to 200°C and elevate dish.

Panasonic:	Combination 4 for 10 minutes
Sharp:	High-Mix 200°C for 8–10 minutes
Sanyo:	Micro/convection 200°C for 8 minutes

To make meringue, beat egg white lightly with a fork. Add icing sugar to form a firm paste resembling royal icing. Roll paste into small balls the size of cherries. Place 6 balls on greaseproof paper, arranging them in a circle. Cook on high (100%) for 1 minute or until firm and dry. Repeat with remaining balls.

To make filling, fold mango and passionfruit pulp through cream. Place pastry on a serving plate. Spread a smooth layer of mango cream over base of pastry. Arrange meringues on top, filling gaps with mango cream. Repeat with remaining meringues, building up circular layers of meringue into a pyramid shape. Chill and serve within 3 hours.

Serves 6–8   M or M/C

Pastry Swirl with French Almond Cream

1 Place cake tin on rolled pastry and cut scalloped border.

2 Cut decorative swirls into top of assembled pastry.

PASTRY SWIRL WITH FRENCH ALMOND CREAM

Pastry
6 sheets prepared puff pastry, 25 cm × 25 cm
⅓ cup water
1 egg, beaten with 1 teaspoon water

Almond Paste
⅓ cup sugar
50 g butter
1 egg
⅓ cup flaked almonds
½ teaspoon almond essence
3 drops vanilla essence
1½ tablespoons rum

French Almond Cream
¾ cup sugar
5 egg yolks
⅓ cup flour, sifted
1¾ cups milk
20 g butter
¼ teaspoon almond essence
1 teaspoon vanilla essence
1 dessertspoon Curacao or orange-flavoured liqueur
4 egg whites
pinch salt
1 tablespoon sugar

To make almond paste, beat sugar and butter until light and fluffy. Beat in egg, almonds, almond and vanilla essences and rum and mix until combined. Place mixture in freezer for 1 hour.

Using a sheet of baking paper, stack three sheets of pastry on top of each other. Reserve remaining pastry sheets. Place a 20 cm round cake tin or bowl in the centre of the top pastry sheet. Using a sharp knife cut a circle through all pastry layers. Remove cake tin.

Roll pastry out gently until it stretches at least 2 cm, making sure it is at least 1 cm thick. Repeat with remaining pastry sheets so you end up with two pastry circles.

Remove almond paste mixture from freezer. Mould in palm of hand into a ball shape. Place almond paste into the centre of one pastry circle. Brush outer edge of pastry with water. Top with second pastry circle pressing firmly to join pastry, and moulding over almond ball to remove excess air.

Place cake tin upsidedown on pastry, with 2 cm showing from beneath tin. Using a sharp knife cut a scalloped border around pastry. Make a hole or 'chimney' with a small metal piping nozzle in centre of pastry mound. Preheat oven to 220°C.

Place completed pastry onto a greased microwave-safe pizza tray. Brush egg and water mixture generously over top and sides of pastry. Refrigerate for 5 minutes. Brush pastry again with egg and water. Using a sharp knife cut decorative swirls into pastry, cutting through egg glaze and about ¼ cm into pastry.

To cook by micro/convection

Panasonic:	Combination 4 for 22 minutes
Sharp:	Low-Mix 200°C for 20 minutes
Sanyo:	Micro/convection 200°C for 20 minutes

To make French almond cream, beat sugar into egg yolks until light and fluffy. Beat in sifted flour. Place milk in a large microwave-safe jug. Cook on high (100%) 3–4 minutes or until milk boils. Gradually beat into egg yolk mixture. Cook on high (100%) for 2 minutes or until mixture begins to boil. Beat in butter, almond and vanilla essences and Curacao until shiny.

Beat egg whites until soft peaks form, add salt and sugar and continue to beat until stiff peaks form. Cool slightly then fold through egg mixture. Refrigerate several hours. When almond pastry is completely cold cut in half horizontally. Sandwich together with French almond cream.

Serves 10–12   M/C

LEMON CREAM PIE

125 g plain biscuits, crushed
60 g butter, softened
4 eggs, separated
¾ cup sugar
grated lemon rind
3 tablespoons lemon juice
1 dessertspoon gelatine
½ cup cream, whipped
yellow food colouring (optional)
lemon rind cut in strips, to garnish

Combine biscuits and butter and press into a 23 cm microwave-safe pie dish. Cook on high (100%) for 2½ minutes. Allow to cool then chill.

Beat egg yolks, ½ cup sugar and 1 teaspoon grated lemon rind until thick and creamy. Warm lemon juice on high (100%) for 45 seconds, then stir in gelatine. Stir this into the egg mixture. Cook on medium-high (70%) for 2–3 minutes, stirring once during cooking. Allow to cool then add whipped cream.

Beat egg whites until soft peaks form. Add remaining sugar and continue to beat to make stiff peaks. Stir in food colouring. Fold egg whites into egg yolk mixture and pour into pie shell. Refrigerate until set. Decorate with thin strips of lemon rind.

Serves 6   M

ORANGE CURACAO CREPES

½ cup sugar
3 egg yolks, beaten
¼ cup flour
½ teaspoon vanilla essence
1 cup milk
1¼ cups cream, whipped
3 oranges, segmented
2 tablespoons Curacao or orange-
  flavoured liqueur
12 prepared crepes

Combine sugar, egg yolks, flour and vanilla with a little of the milk to form a smooth paste. Gradually add remaining milk. Cook on medium (50%) for 4 minutes or until thickened, stirring after each minute. Allow custard to cool.

Fold cream, orange segments and Curacao into cooled custard mixture. Spread mixture over crepes, leaving 1 cm clear around edge. Roll up and serve in pairs.

Serves 6   M

MADEIRA CAKE

175 g butter
¾ cup sugar
grated rind 1 lemon
3 eggs
200 g self-raising flour
2 tablespoons milk
strip candied peel

Preheat oven to 180°C. Grease and line base of 18 cm micro/convection-safe plastic cake container with baking paper. Cream butter, sugar and lemon rind. Beat in eggs, adding a spoonful of flour if the mixture begins to curdle. Fold in remaining flour, then add milk. Pour into prepared container, laying strip of peel on top.

To cook by micro/convection

Panasonic:	Combination 4 for 14–15 minutes
Sharp:	Low-Mix 180°C for 17 minutes
Sanyo:	Micro/convection for 180°C for 7 minutes then convection 180°C for 10 minutes

Serves 6–8   M/C

Left to right: Lemon Cream Pie and Orange Curacao Crepes

Plates Royal Copenhagen Table linen Jaan

COLE PORTERS

First Layer
5 egg yolks, lightly beaten
1 cup sugar
100 g chocolate, melted
140 g walnuts, ground

Second Layer
5 egg whites
1 cup sugar
juice 1 lemon
140 g almonds, ground

Topping
120 g dark chocolate, broken in pieces
25 g copha
2 teaspoons brandy

Combine egg yolks and sugar, beating until thick and fluffy. Fold in melted chocolate and walnuts. Spoon into a lined 20 cm round microwave-safe container. Use baking paper to line.

Beat egg whites and sugar together until soft peaks form. Fold in lemon juice and almonds. Spoon mixture over first layer. Elevate and cook on medium (50%) for 10 minutes. Place a sheet of foil over top of cake (not sides) and cook on medium (50%) for a further 5 minutes. Stand until cool. Turn out and cut into squares.

Melt chocolate and copha in a microwave-safe jug for 1–2 minutes or until melted; stir in brandy. Spoon chocolate mixture over each square and chill until ready to serve.

Makes 10–15   M

HAZELNUT BISCUITS

40 g butter
⅓ cup flour
2 tablespoons caster sugar
60 g ground hazelnuts
1 tablespoon water
extra caster sugar

Rub butter into combined flour and sugar until mixture resembles fine breadcrumbs. Add nuts and water to form a smooth dough. Knead lightly then roll dough onto a lightly floured surface, to form a 15 cm × 25 cm rectangle. Cut into 24 fingers.

Place 12 at a time onto a microwave-safe biscuit tray. Cook, elevated, on high (100%) for 1½–2 minutes. Sprinkle with extra sugar while hot. Cool on tray. Biscuits will crisp on cooling. Repeat with remaining fingers.

Makes 24   M

CHOCOLATE FLORENTINES

60 g butter
¼ cup brown sugar
3 tablespoons flour
¼ cup almonds, finely chopped
¼ cup hazelnuts, finely chopped
3 tablespoons glace cherries, finely chopped
3 tablespoons mixed peel, finely chopped
125 g dark chocolate, melted

Combine butter and sugar in a microwave-safe jug. Cook on high (100%) for 1 minute. Stir in flour and mix until smooth. Add nuts, cherries and peel. Mix to combine.

Cook five florentines at a time arranged in a circle on baking paper. Use one tablespoon of mixture for each florentine and flatten the mixture with a knife. Cook on medium (50%) for 2½ minutes. Cool 3–4 minutes then lift from paper using a spatula. Repeat with remaining mixture.

When cold, spread smooth side of florentines with melted chocolate, using a fork to make wavy lines.

Makes 10   M

GINGERBREAD SHAPES

125 g butter
⅓ cup sugar
⅓ cup golden syrup
3 teaspoons bicarbonate of soda
3 cups flour
½ teaspoon powdered ginger
1 teaspoon cinnamon
1 egg
2 teaspoons vanilla essence

Place butter, sugar and golden syrup in a microwave-safe jug. Cook on high (100%) for 1½–2 minutes or until melted. Cool slightly then add bicarbonate of soda. Add butter mixture to flour and spices. Mix in egg and vanilla to form a soft dough and knead until smooth.

Roll onto a floured surface to 5 mm thickness. Cut into shapes and place 6–8 biscuits on a microwave-safe tray. Cook, elevated, on high (100%) for 1–1½ minutes. Cool on tray. Repeat with remaining biscuits.

Makes 30   M

CHOCOLATE PEPPERMINT SLICE

Base
150 g butter
1 cup sugar
1 teaspoon baking powder
1½ cups flour
2 tablespoons cocoa

Filling
250 g icing sugar
30 g copha, melted
2 tablespoons cream
2 teaspoons peppermint essence
3 drops green food colouring

Topping
100 g chocolate, melted

Preheat oven to 180°C. Cream butter and sugar in food processor. Add baking powder, flour and cocoa and process until combined. Press mixture into a lined 28 cm × 19 cm lamington tray. Use baking paper to line.

To cook by micro/convection

Panasonic:	Combination 4 for 8 minutes
Sharp:	High-Mix 180°C for 7 minutes
Sanyo:	Micro/convection 180°C for 7 minutes

Allow to cool. To make filling, combine all ingredients, mix well and spread evenly over cold base. Top with a thin layer of melted chocolate. Refrigerate until set. Cut into small squares to serve.

Makes 24   M/C

MUESLI SLICE

1 cup brown sugar
½ cup white sugar
1 cup self-raising flour
1½ cups toasted muesli
1 cup Rice Bubbles
1 cup raisins, chopped
½ cup wheatgerm
125 g butter
2 tablespoons honey
1 egg, lightly beaten

In a large bowl combine sugars, flour, muesli, Rice Bubbles, raisins and wheatgerm. In a microwave-safe jug, melt butter and honey on high (100%) for 1 minute, stir and pour over dry ingredients. Mix in egg and press into a 28 cm × 19 cm slice tray. Cook on medium (50%) for 9–11 minutes. Cool, then slice into small rectangles to serve.

Makes 24   M

Pumpkin Almond Bread

Butterdish   David Jones

PUMPKIN ALMOND BREAD

500 g pumpkin, seeds removed
300 g brown sugar
2 eggs
½ cup oil
50 g blanched almonds, chopped
1 teaspoon cinnamon
¾ teaspoon nutmeg
400 g self-raising flour

Cook pumpkin in microwave on high (100%) for 10 minutes. Scrape flesh from skin and puree. Grease and flour a 21 cm × 11 cm microwave-safe loaf tin. Preheat oven to 180°C. Beat together brown sugar, eggs and oil. Mix in remaining ingredients and pour into a prepared loaf tin.

To cook by micro/convection
Panasonic: Convection 180°C for
             5 minutes then
             Combination 4 for
             6 minutes then
             convection 180°C for 35
             minutes
Sharp: Convection 180°C for
             5 minutes then High-Mix
             180°C for 6 minutes
             then convection 180°C
             for 35 minutes

Sanyo: Convection 180°C for
             5 minutes then Micro/
             convection 180°C for
             7 minutes then
             convection 180°C for 35
             minutes

Note: If ends of loaf brown too quickly, shield with foil to prevent burning.

Makes 12–15 slices $\boxed{\text{M/C}}$

CHEWY OAT FINGERS

125 g butter
½ cup brown sugar
3 tablespoons golden syrup
2¾ cups rolled oats
¼ cup flour

Melt butter, sugar and golden syrup on high (100%) for 2 minutes. Stir until sugar is dissolved. Mix in oats and flour. Spread evenly into a 23 cm round microwave-safe flan dish and cook elevated on high (100%) for 5–6 minutes. Cool in the dish.

Makes 24 $\boxed{\text{M}}$

CHERRY NUT SHORTCAKE

2¼ cups flour
⅓ cup caster sugar
1½ teaspoons nutmeg
160 g butter

Topping
200 g glace cherries, quartered
100 g slivered almonds
50 g walnuts, roughly chopped
½ cup honey

Preheat oven to 200°C. Place flour, sugar, nutmeg and butter in food processor and process until mixed. Press into a greased and lined 21 cm round tray. Use baking paper to line.

To cook by micro/convection
Panasonic: Combination 4 for
             8 minutes
Sharp: High-Mix 200°C for
             6 minutes
Sanyo: Micro/convection 200°C
             for 6 minutes

To make topping, combine cherries, almonds, walnuts and honey. Cook on high (100%) for 8–10 minutes or until mixture becomes spreadable. Spread evenly over shortcake. Stand until set. Cut into wedges to serve.

Makes 24 $\boxed{\text{M/C}}$

COFFEE BRANDY SLICE

Base
100 g butter
½ cup sugar
1 egg
1 tablespoon instant coffee
½ teaspoon brandy
1 ¾ cups flour
1 teaspoon baking powder

Filling
50 g butter, melted
1 tablespoon golden syrup
1 tablespoon brown sugar
⅔ cup condensed milk
1 teaspoon brandy
1 tablespoon cornflour

Topping
100 g chocolate, melted

Preheat oven to 180°C. Cream butter and sugar together in a bowl. Beat in egg, coffee, brandy, flour and baking powder. Knead until smooth. Press into a lined 28 cm × 19 cm microwave-safe lamington tin.

Combine all filling ingredients, mixing until smooth. Spread over coffee base.

To cook by micro/convection

Panasonic:	Combination 4 for 13 minutes
Sharp:	High-Mix 180°C for 12 minutes
Sanyo:	Micro/convection 180°C for 12 minutes

Spread with thin layer of melted chocolate. Allow to cool. Serve cut in log shapes.

Makes 24   M/C

COCONUT SLICE

Base
125 g butter
½ cup sugar
1 egg, lightly beaten
1 ½ cups flour

Topping
½ cup raspberry jam
1 ½ cups desiccated coconut
1 egg
½ cup sugar

Preheat oven to 200°C. Cream butter and sugar together in a bowl. Beat in egg and flour until combined. Press into a greased and lined 28 cm × 19 cm slice tray. Use baking paper to line.

To cook by micro/convection

Panasonic:	Combination 4 for 7 minutes
Sharp:	High-Mix 200°C for 7 minutes
Sanyo:	Micro/convection for 5 minutes, then convection 200°C for 5 minutes

To make topping, spread jam over hot base. Combine coconut, egg and sugar and sprinkle over jam.

To cook by micro/convection

Panasonic:	Combination 4 for 12 minutes
Sharp:	High-Mix 200°C for 12 minutes
Sanyo:	Micro/convection 200°C 12 minutes

Cook until golden. Allow to cool completely. Cut into squares to serve.

Makes 24   M/C

CHOCOLATE ROUGH SLICE

1 cup sugar
250 g butter
2 cups self-raising flour
1 tablespoon coconut
1 tablespoon cocoa
1–2 tablespoons milk

Topping
2 cups icing sugar
2 cups desiccated coconut
4 tablespoons milk
1 ½ tablespoons cocoa

Line the base of a 19 cm × 28 cm slice tray with baking paper. Preheat oven to 180°C. Beat sugar and butter until fluffy. Mix in flour, coconut, cocoa and enough milk to form a soft dough. Press into slice tray.

To cook by micro/convection

Panasonic:	Combination 4 for 12 minutes
Sharp:	High-Mix 180°C for 10 minutes
Sanyo:	Micro/convection 180°C for 10 minutes

To make topping, combine icing sugar, coconut, milk and cocoa. Spread over cake base while still warm. Chill until set. Cut into squares to serve.

Makes 20   M/C

Clockwise from top left: Coffee Brandy Slice, Coconut Slice, Cole Porters, Chocolate Rough Slice and Cherry Nut Shortcake

Left to right: Pickled Mushrooms, Kiwi Fruit Jam, Watermelon Rind in Ginger Syrup, Capsicum Relish, Apple and Capsicum Chutney, Pink Apple Butter, Pistachio Colettes, Cherry Nut Chocolates, Hazelnut Petits Fours, Modelling Dough Truffles, Turkish Delight,

SPECIAL TREATS

This section contains goodies for the entire family.
Try sweets such as Turkish Delight, Rocky Road or
Nut Brittle; savouries like Pickled Mushrooms and
Capsicum Relish; or useful recipes for playdough
and drying flowers. We have included a selection of
festive food, ideal for Christmas or for those extra
special dinner parties.

CHOCOLATE LIQUEUR PRUNES

500 g prunes, pitted
½ cup port or favourite liqueur
200 g dark chocolate, broken into pieces
15 g copha

Soak prunes in port or liqueur overnight. Melt chocolate and copha on high (100%) for 1½–2 minutes or until melted. Dip drained prunes in chocolate and place on baking paper to set.

Makes approximately 30

CREAMY FUDGE

165 g butter
1 cup blanched almonds, chopped
2 cups sugar
1 cup evaporated milk
200 g white chocolate, broken into pieces
1 cup white marshmallows
1 teaspoon vanilla essence

Place 40 g butter in a shallow microwave-safe dish. Cook on high (100%) for 30 seconds or until melted. Add almonds and cook on high (100%) for 4 minutes or until toasted.

Combine sugar, 125 g butter and evaporated milk in a microwave-safe jug. Cook on medium-high (70%) for 19 minutes, stirring frequently. Add chocolate and marshmallows. Beat using a wooden spoon until melted. Add toasted almonds and vanilla. Beat until fudge thickens.

Pour into a greased slice tray 24 cm × 13 cm. Refrigerate until set. Serve cut into squares.

Makes 36

NUT BRITTLE

⅓ cup water
1¼ cups caster sugar
½ teaspoon cream of tartar
60 g butter
¾ cup flaked almonds

Combine water, sugar, cream of tartar and butter in a microwave-safe bowl. Cook on high (100%) for 3–4 minutes or until butter has melted. Add almonds, stir and cook on high (100%) for 6–8 minutes or until golden brown.

Press into a greased pie dish. Chill until almost set. Cut into small diamond shapes and chill.

Makes 30

MINT CREAM DELIGHTS

1½ cups sugar
1½ cups thickened cream
1 tablespoon gelatine
3 tablespoons Creme de Menthe
¼ cup icing sugar

Combine sugar, cream, gelatine and Creme-de-Menthe in a microwave-safe jug. Cook on high (100%) for 5 minutes then stir. Cook on medium-high (70%) for 8 minutes. Pour mixture into a lightly greased slice tray 24 cm by 13 cm.

Sprinkle with icing sugar and refrigerate until set. Cut into squares to serve.

Makes 36

TURKISH DELIGHT

2 cups sugar
3 cups water
4 tablespoons gelatine
¼ teaspoon tartaric acid
⅔ cup cornflour
1½ cups icing sugar
¼ teaspoon rose water
pink food colouring

Coating
¾ cup icing sugar
¾ cup cornflour

Place sugar, 1½ cups water and the gelatine in a 2 litre microwave-safe bowl. Cook on high (100%) for 5 minutes, then stir until sugar is dissolved. Cook on high (100%) for 16–18 minutes. Add tartaric acid and stir.

Combine cornflour and icing sugar, mixing to a smooth paste with ½ cup water. Cook remaining 1 cup water on high (100%) for 2 minutes. Add cornflour mixture, stirring well. Cook on high (100%) for 5–6 minutes or until mixture thickens, stirring once.

Blend in sugar syrup and cook on high (100%) for 8–9 minutes or until transparent and a very pale fawn colour. Add rose water and colouring.

Pour into a lightly oiled 24 cm × 13 cm dish. Stand for several hours until set. Cut into 3 cm cubes with a wet knife. Toss squares in combined icing sugar and cornflour to coat.

Note: Rose water is readily available from delicatessens and chemists.

Makes 24

HAZELNUT PETITS FOURS

Cases
100 g cooking chocolate
20 g copha
16 petits fours cases

Filling
20 g butter
40 g hazelnuts, finely chopped
100 g cream cheese, softened
1 tablespoon orange juice
grated chocolate, to decorate

Melt chocolate and copha on high (100%) for 1–2 minutes or until melted. Place a small quantity of chocolate in each petits fours case and with a small paint brush, coat base and sides of cases with chocolate. Refrigerate to set.

To make filling, soften butter on high (100%) for 20 seconds. Add nuts, cream cheese and orange juice and chill. Pipe filling into chocolate cases. Chill and decorate with grated chocolate.

Makes 16

CHOCOLATE COATED CANDIED PEEL

2 oranges
water
caster sugar
375 g dark chocolate
1 tablespoon copha

Quarter oranges and remove skins. Remove all white pith. Trim each quarter of peel into fine strips the size of a small French fry.

Place all peel in a microwave-safe jug, cover with cold water. Cook on high (100%) for 5 minutes, then drain. Repeat this process three times. Weigh the peel and return it to the jug with an equal quantity of sugar. Cover with cold water and cook on high (100%) for 30 minutes. Remove peel and drain on a rack for 2 hours.

Roll peel in caster sugar. Leave to dry completely for 2 hours. Melt chocolate and copha together on high (100%) for 2 minutes. Coat peel with melted chocolate and place on baking paper to set.

Makes 40

Glassware Orrefors

MARBLED ALMOND TRUFFLES

¼ cup icing sugar
70 g ground almonds
2 tablespoons custard powder
2 teaspoons brandy
315 g white chocolate, broken in pieces
15 whole almonds, shelled
125 g dark chocolate, broken in pieces

Combine icing sugar, ground almonds, custard powder and brandy. Place 190 g white chocolate in a microwave-safe jug. Cook on high (100%) for 1½ minutes or until melted. Stir in almond mixture. Refrigerate until firm.

Mould 1 teaspoon of mixture around each whole almond, rolling in the palm of your hand to make a smooth ball. Refrigerate.

Melt dark and remaining 125 g white chocolate in separate bowls for 1½ minutes on high (100%). Dip truffles in white chocolate. Using the tip of a sharp knife, gently spread dark chocolate to form a marbled effect. Place on a tray lined with baking paper to set.

Makes 15   M

CHOCOLATE HAZELNUT TRUFFLES

125 g ground hazelnuts
1 cup icing sugar
1 egg white
¼ cup cream
2 tablespoons Tia Maria
375 g dark chocolate, broken in pieces

Decoration
cocoa
desiccated coconut
crushed nuts

Combine ground hazelnuts with icing sugar. Add egg white, cream and Tia Maria and mix well. In a microwave-safe jug, melt chocolate on high (100%) for 2 minutes or until melted. Add hazelnut mixture and stir to combine. Refrigerate until firm. Roll teaspoonsful of mixture into balls, then roll one-third of the balls in cocoa to coat, one-third in coconut and one-third in crushed nuts.

Makes approximately 30   M

Top to bottom: Chocolate Hazelnut Truffles, Hazelnut Petits Fours, Pistachio Colettes, Turkish Delight, Cherry Nut Chocolates, Creamy Fudge, Marbled Almond Truffles, Nut Brittle

PISTACHIO COLETTES

Colette Cases
125 g dark cooking chocolate, broken into pieces
24 small petits fours cases (see Note)

Filling
150 g dark cooking chocolate, broken in pieces
60 g butter
2 egg yolks
1 tablespoon rum
120 mL cream, whipped
chopped pistachio nuts, to decorate

To make cases, melt chocolate on high (100%) for 1–2 minutes or until melted. Using a paint brush, paint the bottom and sides of petits fours cases. Refrigerate until set.

To make filling, place chocolate and butter in a microwave-safe jug. Cook on high (100%) for 1½ minutes or until melted. Stir egg yolks and rum into chocolate mixture and beat until smooth. Cool mixture and fold through whipped cream. Pipe chocolate cream mixture into petits fours cases. Sprinkle with chopped pistachio nuts and refrigerate until set.

Note: Petits fours cases are made of paper and are readily available at supermarkets.
Makes 24

ROCKY ROAD

375 g cooking chocolate
15 g copha
1 cup crushed nuts
½ cup glace cherries, halved
250 g pink and white marshmallows, chopped in half

Break chocolate into pieces. Place chocolate and copha into a microwave-safe jug and cook on high (100%) for 2 minutes or until chocolate melts.

Line a loaf container with foil. Add nuts, cherries and marshmallows to chocolate. Stir to combine all ingredients well and pour into lined container. Refrigerate until set. Remove from container and serve cut into squares.

Serves 20

CHERRY NUT CHOCOLATES

375 g dark chocolate, broken into pieces
30 g copha
1 teaspoon instant coffee
¾ cup toasted desiccated coconut
185 g glace cherries
185 g cashew nuts, chopped
icing sugar, to decorate

Place chocolate and copha in a microwave-safe jug and cook on high (100%) for 2 minutes or until chocolate is melted. Reserve one-quarter of this mixture. Into remaining three-quarters, stir coffee, coconut, cherries and nuts and pour into a foil-lined slice tray 14 cm × 25 cm. Smooth down and spread reserved chocolate-copha mix over top. Chill to set.

Cut into 5 cm squares. Place a sheet of greaseproof paper diagonally over each square, to protect one half of chocolate. Sprinkle uncovered half with icing sugar.

Makes 36

MERINGUE PETITS FOURS

1 egg white, lightly beaten
250 g icing sugar

Choose Three of the Following Flavourings:
- *1 teaspoon instant coffee dissolved in hot water*
- *rose essence with pink food colouring*
- *mint essence with green food colouring*
- *finely chopped crystallised or stem ginger*
- *1 teaspoon cocoa dissolved in hot water*

Combine egg white and icing sugar to form a firm paste until mixture resembles royal icing. Divide mixture into three parts. Knead one of the above flavourings into each mixture, adding more icing if necessary.

Using a surface dusted with icing sugar, roll each mixture to form a 1 cm wide sausage. Break off small pieces and roll into the shape of a pea. Repeat with remaining mixture.

Place 10 at a time in a circle on baking paper. Cook on high (100%) for 1 minute or until dry and firm. Repeat with remaining balls. Serve in petits fours cases or sandwich two together using flavoured cream.

Makes 60

PINK APPLE BUTTER

1 kg red apples, cored and chopped
juice 1 lemon
1 tablespoon water
nutmeg
cinnamon
sugar
red food colouring

Cook apples and lemon juice in a large microwave-safe bowl on high (100%) for 15–20 minutes or until fruit is very soft. Place apples and water in a food processor and process until pureed.

Measure puree. Add a sprinkle of nutmeg and cinnamon and ½ cup of sugar for each cup of puree. Cook on high (100%) for 15–20 minutes or until mixture is thick, stirring several times during cooking. If a deeper pink is desired add a few drops of red food colouring.

Pour into warm, sterilised jars and cool before sealing.

Makes 1 cup

WATERMELON RIND IN GINGER SYRUP

500 g watermelon rind
3 cups sugar
1 lemon, cut in half and thinly sliced
50 g grated fresh ginger root

To prepare rind, peel the green outer skin from the melon and remove pink flesh from the other side. Cut green rind into 5 cm strips, place in a dish and cover with cold water for at least 12 hours.

Drain water from rind. Pour 2 cups fresh water over it and cook on high (100%) for 15 minutes or until rind is just tender. Remove and reserve rind.

To the water add sugar, lemon and ginger. Cook on high (100%) for 25 minutes, stirring several times during cooking. Add watermelon rind to syrup and cook on high (100%) for 15 minutes. Remove rind and lemon and pack into warm sterilised jars. Cook syrup on high (100%) for a further 5 minutes. Pour over rind and seal.

Store leftover syrup in a spare bottle and seal. Use for a quick topping over ice cream.

Makes 2 cups

LEMON SPREAD

80 g butter
¾ cup sugar
2 teaspoons lemon rind, grated
¼ cup lemon juice
3 eggs, lightly beaten

Place butter and sugar in a microwave-safe jug. Cook on high (100%) for 1 minute. Stir and cook for a further 2 minutes. Stir again and cook on high (100%) for 1 minute.

Add rind, juice and eggs, blending well. Cook on high (100%) for 4 minutes, stirring after each minute. Pour into sterilised jars and seal.

Makes 1 cup ☐M

Clockwise from left: Pink Apple Butter, Apple and Capsicum Chutney, Watermelon Rind in Ginger Syrup, Capsicum Relish, Pickled Mushrooms, Kiwi Fruit Jam, Tamarillo Relish, Lemon Spread

KIWI FRUIT JAM

750 g kiwi fruit, peeled and roughly
*   chopped*
¼ cup water
juice 1 lemon
2 cups sugar
few drops green food colouring (optional)

Cook kiwi fruit and water on high (100%) for 7–10 minutes or until fruit is pulped — time varies depending on ripeness of fruit. Add lemon juice and sugar, stir, cook on high (100%) for 10–15 minutes or until jam sets when tested. Add food colouring if using to give the jam a good green colour. Pour into warmed sterilised jars and allow jam to cool before sealing.

Makes 2 cups ☐M

PICKLED MUSHROOMS

1200 mL white wine vinegar
2 onions, finely chopped
2 bay leaves
2 tablespoons black peppercorns
2 tablespoons coriander seeds
750 g small, very fresh mushrooms

Place vinegar, onion, bay leaves, peppercorns and coriander seeds in a microwave-safe jug and cook on high (100%) for 10 minutes. Strain and return liquid to jug. Add mushrooms and cook on high (100%) for 2–2½ minutes or until mushrooms are tender, but not soft.

Pack mushrooms firmly into sterilised jars, pouring liquid to within 0.5 cm of top. Seal and store in a cool dark place for 3 weeks before using.

Makes 2 × 600 mL jars ☐M

Glass bowl Holmegaard

CAPSICUM RELISH

2 red capsicums, cut into thin strips
2 large onions, thinly sliced
1 cup white vinegar
1 cup brown sugar
½ teaspoon ground ginger
1 fresh chilli, finely chopped
pinch cayenne pepper

Place capsicums and onions in a large microwave-safe bowl. Cover and cook on high (100%) for 10 minutes, stirring once during cooking. Add remaining ingredients and stir. Cook on high (100%) for 45 minutes, stirring every 15 minutes. Pour into warm, sterilised jars. Cool before sealing.

Makes 2 cups

TAMARILLO RELISH

500 g tamarillos, halved
2 apples, cored and roughly chopped
2 onions, peeled, halved and sliced
1 teaspoon ground ginger
1 ½ cups brown sugar
1 cup malt vinegar

Cook tamarillos on high (100%) for 5 minutes. Using tongs, peel skin from tamarillos. Combine tamarillos, apples, onions and ginger in a microwave-safe jug. Cook on high (100%) for 10 minutes or until fruit is very soft. Add sugar and vinegar, stir. Cook on high (100%) for 30 minutes or until relish is thick. Stir and pour into warm sterilised jars. Allow to cool before sealing.

Makes 3½–4 cups M

ORANGE CHUTNEY

4 oranges
2 apples, cored and chopped
1 tablespoon chopped ginger in syrup
1 tablespoon raisins
1 fresh chilli, finely chopped
freshly ground black pepper
1 ½ cups brown sugar
¼ cup honey
1 cup white or cider vinegar

Peel oranges as thinly as possible and reserve peel. Remove pith and pips from orange flesh and discard. Shred peel. Roughly chop orange flesh. Place orange flesh, peel, apples, ginger, raisins, chilli and pepper in a microwave-safe jug. Cook on high (100%) for 10 minutes or until fruit is very soft.

Add sugar, honey and vinegar. Cook on high (100%) for 25 minutes or until mixture thickens, stirring 2–3 times during cooking. Pour chutney into warm, sterilised jars. Allow to cool before sealing.

Makes 2 cups M

Dried Flowers and potpourri

APPLE AND CAPSICUM CHUTNEY

50 g fresh ginger root, peeled
6–8 apples, peeled and cored
2 capsicums (red or green), seeded
1 onion, peeled
1 fresh chilli, chopped and seeded
1 cup raisins
1 cup malt vinegar
1 cup water
juice and grated rind 2 lemons

Place ginger, apples, capsicums, onions and chilli in food processor and roughly chop. Place all ingredients in a large microwave-safe dish. Cook on high (100%) for 30–40 minutes or until chutney is thick. Pour chutney into warm sterilised jars. Allow to cool before sealing.

Makes 5–6 cups

DRYING FLOWERS

Many flowers can be successfully dried in the microwave. Fresh, half-opened flowers with thick petals produce the best results. Carnations, roses, pansies, daffodils or chrysanthemums are ideal.

6 cups silica gel (or new kitty litter)
selection of flowers
toothpicks
florists' wire
florists' tape

If silica gel is granulated, process in food processor until it becomes a fine powder.

Cut stem from each flower just below the base of the flower. Place ½ cup silica gel into six cups. Sit flowers on top. Opening petals with toothpick, gently sprinkle gel in between petals, to thoroughly cover flowers. Tap cups on bench to evenly distribute gel powder.

Cook 4–6 cups at a time on high (100%) for 1½ minutes. Check degree of dryness. If petals are still soft, cook on high (100%) for 30 seconds at a time until dry. The time taken depends on the size and moisture content of the flower.

Tip gel from top of flower, leaving flower to sit in the remaining hot gel for several minutes. Remove flowers, gently shake off any excess powder. Remove toothpick from flowers, insert florists' wire through flower base, drawing through top of flower. Form a small hook in wire at top of flower, gently draw wire back down until hooked in flower. Cover base of flower and wire with florists' tape.

TO MAKE POTPOURRI

Dry a selection of baby rose buds or selected flowers. Sprinkle with perfumed or fragrant oil.

MODELLING DOUGH

1 cup flour
¾ cup water combined with food colouring of your choice
2 tablespoons cream of tartar
1 tablespoon oil
¼ cup salt

Combine all ingredients and mix well. Cook on medium (50%) for 6–7 minutes, stirring every minute. The mixture will leave the sides of the dish when cooked. Store in an airtight container.

STRAWBERRY TREE

small decorative or terracotta pot filled with sand
30 cm piece wooden dowelling, painted
polystyrene ball
ribbon, to decorate
375 g dark chocolate
15 g copha
500 g strawberries, washed, hulls left on

Fill a small, decorative terracotta pot with sand. Insert one end of the dowelling into the sand, and the other end into the base of a polystyrene ball. Decorate dowelling with ribbon and hide sand with miniature parcels or pine cones.

Melt chocolate and copha together on high (100%) for 2 minutes. Dip tips of strawberries into melted chocolate to coat half of each strawberry. Place on baking paper to set.

Push a toothpick into the hull end of each strawberry, then carefully push into polystyrene ball, positioning strawberries as close together as possible. Decorate with ribbons.

Use as a table centrepiece.

COFFEE LIQUEUR

4 cups sugar
½ cup instant coffee
3 cups water
¼ teaspoon salt
2 cups brandy
1 cup rum
1 tablespoon vanilla essence

Combine sugar, coffee, water and salt in a microwave-safe jug. Cook on high (100%) for 5 minutes. Stir until sugar is dissolved. Cook on high (100%) for 10–12 minutes.

Skim any froth from the top. Stir in brandy, rum and vanilla. Mix well, cool and pour into sterilised bottles. Store in a cool place for 2 weeks before using.

Makes 6½ cups

BROCCOLI AND CHERRY TOMATO WREATH

500 g broccoli
10 cherry tomatoes

Cut broccoli into small flowerets and arrange with tomatoes in a 20 cm ring container so heads of flowerets face towards outside of container with tomatoes in between. Cook covered on high (100%) for 4 minutes. Remove cover and invert food onto serving plate.

Serves 6

> Steam towels for a touch of after-dinner luxury. Place saturated hand towels, wrung out, in a freeze bag. Cook on high (100%) for 1 minute.

ORIENTAL TURKEY

3 tablespoons soy sauce
2 tablespoons honey
1 teaspoon finely chopped fresh ginger
   root
1 clove garlic, crushed
1 chilli, finely chopped
3 kg turkey

Stuffing
1 onion, roughly chopped
½ teaspoon finely chopped fresh ginger
   root
40 g butter
8 slices wholegrain bread, crumbed
2 tablespoons chopped fresh parsley
1 tablespoon chopped fresh chives
freshly ground black pepper

Mix together first five ingredients and place 2 tablespoons in cavity of turkey. Tie the legs of the bird together with string and tuck wings under. Place bird and remaining soy sauce mixture in an oven bag. Toss so that the baste coats the bird. Tie the end of the bag loosely with string and place breast side down in an ovenproof glass or ceramic baking dish on wire elevation rack.

To cook by micro/convection
Turn bird over halfway through cooking

Panasonic:	Combination 4 for 20 minutes/500 g
Sharp:	High-Mix 200°C for 16 minutes/500 g
Sanyo:	Micro/convection 200°C for 10 minutes/500 g

To make the stuffing, cook onion, ginger and butter together on high (100%) for 2 minutes. Add remaining ingredients and mix to combine. Press stuffing into a 29 cm × 19 cm microwave-safe slice tin. Baste stuffing with 1 tablespoon of juices from the turkey. Halfway through cooking, place stuffing on turntable to cook.

Serve stuffing and turkey separately.

Serves 6-8 　　　　　　　 M/C

AMARETTO BOMBE

4 cups self-raising flour
pinch salt
90 g butter
1 ¼ cups milk
¼ teaspoon mixed spice (microwave
   only)
½ cup Amaretto liqueur
2 cups cream, whipped
1 × 250 g punnet strawberries, washed
   and hulled
icing sugar

Combine flour and salt. Rub butter into flour until mixture resembles breadcrumbs. Add milk, mixing until mixture forms a soft dough. Knead lightly. Form into a large round, 16 cm in diameter.

Preheat browning dish for 6-8 minutes on high (100%). Sprinkle dough mixture with mixed spice. Add to browning dish, cook on high (100%) for 7-8 minutes. Stand until cold. Alternatively, cook by micro/convection (see below).

To cook by micro/convection
Preheat oven to 220°C. Place round on a greased microwave-safe metal tray, brush lightly with milk.

Panasonic:	Combination 4 for 3 minutes then convection at 220°C for 15-17 minutes
Sharp:	High-Mix at 220°C for 2 minutes then convection at 220°C for 15-17 minutes
Sanyo:	Micro/convection at 220°C for 2 minutes then on convection at 220°C for 15 minutes

When cold cut into halves horizontally. Sprinkle cut side of both halves with Amaretto liqueur. Sandwich bombe together with half the whipped cream and strawberries. Use remaining cream and strawberries to decorate. Sprinkle with icing sugar just before serving.

Serves 8 　　　 M 　or　 M/C

WHITE CHRISTMAS

250 g copha, roughly chopped
2 cups coconut
1 cup icing sugar
3 tablespoons non-fat dried milk powder
¼ cup glace cherries, chopped
¼ cup crystallised ginger, chopped
½ cup dried apricots, chopped
¼ cup glace pineapple, chopped
½ cup mixed peel

Place copha in a large microwave-safe jug. Cook on high (100%) for 5-6 minutes or until melted. Add remaining ingredients, combining thoroughly. Press into a foil-lined lamington tray. Refrigerate until set and cut into bars to serve.

Makes 24 　　　　　　　 M

MOIST FRUIT CAKE

1 kg mixed fruit
1 cup brown sugar
200 g butter
1 teaspoon cinnamon
2 tablespoons water or alcohol of your
   choice
4 eggs
1 dessertspoon Parisian essence
1 cup self-raising flour

Topping
1 cup apricot jam
glazed cherries, halved
pecan nuts

Combine first five ingredients in a large microwave-safe casserole dish. Cook covered on high (100%) for 7 minutes, then stir. Cool completely, then add remaining ingredients, stirring well.

Line a 20 cm round microwave-safe plastic container with baking paper. Place a strip of foil around outside upright edge of container. Pour mixture into container and cook, elevated, on medium-low (30%) for 25 minutes.

Remove from oven and test. If further cooking is required, remove foil and cook for 5 minutes on high (100%). While cake is warm, brush top with melted apricot jam. Arrange cherries and pecans on top, seal with extra jam. Cool before removing from container.

Serves 8　　　　　　　　M

CHRISTMAS PUDDING

250 g butter
250 g brown sugar
4 eggs
1 kg mixed fruit
1 cup stewed apple
1 cup flour
1 ½ cups soft breadcrumbs
1 teaspoon cinnamon
½ teaspoon nutmeg
½ teaspoon ground ginger
½ teaspoon allspice
2 tablespoons Parisian essence
½ cup sweet sherry
1 tablespoon golden syrup

Cream butter and sugar then add remaining ingredients in the order listed. Grease and flour a microwave-safe jug or pudding bowl. Pour in mixture and cook on medium-low or defrost (30%) for 38 minutes. Place a 4 cm collar of foil around top of pudding bowl and cook for a further 15–20 minutes on medium-low (30%).

Serves 8　　　　　　　　M

Clockwise from centre top: Moist Fruit Cake, Strawberry Tree, Chocolate Hazelnut Truffles, Cherry Nut Chocolates, Amaretto Bombe, Oriental Turkey and Broccoli and Cherry Tomato Wreath

GLOSSARY

BACON RASHERS: bacon slices.

BEEF

Mince: ground beef.
Blade: cut of beef next to the shoulder blade, ideal for hot pots and casseroles.
Chuck: cut of beef taken from between the neck and shoulder blade, ideal for hot pots and casseroles.
Fillet steak: piece taken from the underside of the rump and sirloin, which has little fat.
Rump steak: cut of beef taken from the hinder part of the animal behind the loin.
Scotch fillet: also called ribeye; cut of beef with some of the best muscle meat, taken from near the ribs. It can be roasted in one piece or cut into steaks.

BICARBONATE OF SODA: baking soda, an ingredient in baking powder.

BREADCRUMBS

Soft: fresh breadcrumbs, made with one or two day old bread in a blender or food processor.
Dry: commercial packaged breadcrumbs.

BUTTER: use salted butter unless otherwise specified.

CABBAGE: use green cabbage (also known as roundhead or common cabbage) unless otherwise specified e.g. red cabbage or white cabbage.

CALAMARI: squid. Prepare as directed according to a particular recipe.

CAPSICUM: sweet peppers, red and green.

CHEESE

Tasty: use mature Cheddar.

CHICKEN: recipes specify exact weight required e.g. 1.2 kg.

CHILLI: use fresh chillies where specified, with great care. Rubber gloves can protect the skin from burning but make sure you never touch your eyes while preparing chilli. As the seeds are the hottest part, these can be removed and discarded if preferred.

COPHA: a form of purified coconut oil, also sold as coconut butter, Copha Butter and Kremelta (registered trademarks).

COCONUT, DESICCATED: shredded coconut.

CORNFLOUR: cornstarch.

CREAM: also known as single, light or coffee cream.
Thickened cream: double, heavy or whipping cream.
Sour cream: soured or dairy sour cream. Also available in a fat-reduced form which has fewer calories.

EGGPLANT: aubergine.

ESSENCE: extract.

FLOUR: Use plain or all-purpose flour unless otherwise stated.
Self-raising flour: all-purpose flour to which baking powder has been added in the proportions of 1 cup (125 g) flour: 1 teaspoon (10 g) baking powder.

GINGER
Fresh ginger root: available at a green grocer's or fruiterer's; usually peeled and chopped before using.
Powdered ginger: ground ginger, available in spice jars.

GOLDEN SYRUP: maple or pancake syrup can be used instead.

HERBS: our recipes specify whether to use fresh or dried herbs, but if you need to replace fresh herbs with dried, the ratio is one to four: one teaspoon of dried to four teaspoons (one tablespoon) of fresh herbs.

LAMB
Chump chops: chops cut from the chump section located between the leg and the loin.
Cutlets: chops cut from the rib loin; can be grilled, fried or roasted.
Leg chops: chops taken from the top of the leg.
Loin chops: standard cut of lamb, veal or pork, cut from the upper flank and including the lower ribs.
Rack of lamb: cutlets from rib loin section still joined together.
Shanks: pieces cut from the top part of the legs.

MIXED SPICE: finely ground spice combination, including allspice, nutmeg and cinnamon; used to flavour cakes and buns.

MUESLI: granola.

OIL: use a vegetable or olive oil, unless otherwise specified.

PARISIAN ESSENCE: flavouring extract available in supermarkets and delicatessens. Can be replaced with Hansell's Gravy Browner (registered trademark).

PAW PAW: papaya or papaw.

PIMENTO: allspice.

PIMIENTO: canned or bottled type of chilli pepper.

PORK
Butterfly chop or steak: boned, rind removed loin chop or steak, split in half and opened out.
Fillet: boned, rind removed piece cut from the underside of the rump and sirloin.
Medallions: rind removed, boned, round pieces taken from the loin.
Spareribs: meat cut from the ribs still containing rib bones.
Steaks: pieces cut from the leg or rump across the grain of the muscle.
Tenderloin: a very tender strip of meat, part of the loin under the ribs.

PRAWN: shrimp.

PUMPKIN: use any type.

ROCK MELON: also known as ogen melon and cantaloupe.

SAUCES
Hoi Sin sauce: Chinese sauce made from onions, garlic and salted black beans.
Soy sauce: made from soya beans; a great variety is available, especially from Asian foodstores. Experiment to find which one you prefer to use with different foods.

SHALLOTS: very small white onions also known as scallions and spring onions.
Spring onions: larger, white-bulbed sweet onions.

STOCK CUBE: bouillon cube; can be replaced with one teaspoon powdered stock or bouillon.

SUGAR
Caster: fine white granulated sugar.
Raw: brown granulated sugar.
Brown: soft, moist sugar.
Icing: confectioner's or powdered sugar.

SULTANAS: seedless white raisins.

TOMATO PASTE: also known as tomato concentrate.

TOMATO SAUCE: tomato ketchup.

VEAL
Chops: taken from the loin and the ribs.
Cutlets: taken from the loin and the ribs.
Escalopes: thin slices, often coated in breadcrumbs and fried.

WHOLEMEAL: wholewheat.

YOGHURT: use natural or unflavoured yoghurt.

ZUCCHINI: courgette.

EQUIPMENT AND TERMS
CAN, CANNED: tin, tinned.

CRUSHED: minced, pressed.

FRYING PAN: skillet.

GRILL: broil.

GREASEPROOF PAPER: waxproof paper.

LAMINGTON TIN: oven tray 4 cm (1 ½ inches) deep. Grease and use as a biscuit or cake tin.

PAPER CASES: paper baking cases or cups; also available as petits fours (type of French small cake) cases.

PAPER TOWEL: absorbent kitchen paper towel.

PLASTIC WRAP: cling film.

PUNNET: small box or basket containing about 250 g (8 oz) of fruit.

SANDWICH TIN: layer cake pan.

SEEDED: stoned or pitted — stone removed and discarded.

SPRING-FORM CAKE TIN: spring pan or loose-bottomed cake tin.

SWISS ROLL TIN: jelly roll pan.

INDEX